The Matter of the Facts

THE MATTER OF THE FACTS

On Invention and Interpretation

Miguel Tamen

STANFORD UNIVERSITY PRESS

STANFORD, CALIFORNIA

2000

Library of Congress Cataloging-in-Publication Data

Tamen, Miguel
The matter of the facts : on invention and interpretation / Miguel Tamen
   p.   cm.
Includes bibliographical references and index.
ISBN 0-8047-3432-1 (alk. paper)
1. Literature—History and criticism—Theory, etc.   2. Criticism.
3. Hermeneutics.   I. Title.

PN81.T3167   2000
801'.95—dc21   00-057325

This book is printed on acid-free, archival-quality paper.

Original printing 2000

Last figure below indicates year of this printing:
09   08   07   06   05   04   03   02   01   00

Designed and typeset in 10/15 Revival by John Feneron

Contents

. . . aquilo que mais val
que então se entende melhor
quando mais perdido for

. . . that which is valued the most,
thus better understood
when more completely lost
　　—Luís de Camões, "Sobre os rios"

Introduction: This Book

This book started out as a historical study, *The Invention of Interpretation*. Then it ambitiously became *Invention in Interpretation*. When I realized it could not end up as a theory of reading, the book, finally, acquired its present title by becoming an investigation, as well as an instance, of what affects both interpretations and theories of reading. The first title grew out of my increasing discomfort concerning "the hermeneutic claim to universality" (to borrow, with a different sense, the phrase from Jürgen Habermas):[1] the presupposition that interpretation is *the* problem of language and that hermeneutics is its organon. Such a presupposition has led authors like Georges Gusdorf to find hermeneutics all over the world and all over time—to speak, for example of "the Golden Age of Alexandrian hermeneutics"[2] while of course knowing very well that the designation is historically inadequate.

My original aim (which, as I did find out, was hardly original) was simple enough: to show that before Kant there was no interpretation (let alone a hermeneutics). Of course, I was planning on attenuating the paradox through the study of some pre-Kantian varieties of exegesis, to be crowned by a final chapter on the lexical coincidence between *Verstand* (the faculty of the Understanding) and *Verstehen* (interpretation), as well as on an altogether new doctrine of the Understanding that, after Schleiermacher, gave hermeneutics its philosophical dignity. I found some confirmation of my original intention in Manfred Frank's work, namely in his remark that "hermeneutics ... is a Romantic invention,"[3] albeit, I thought, with a crucial difference that had to do with Kant's role. In fact, even at that stage, I felt reluctant to endorse Frank's avowedly "extremely simplified" description,[4] according to which "after the breakdown of the axioms of the universality of reason, the Romantic theory of language was compelled to explain the trans-individual validity of language in a different way than on the basis that language, because of its natural transparency to reason, must also itself be rational (and universal)."[5] Now, more than ever, my contention (which persists in what has become Chapter 4) is that Kant already had few illusions as to the "rationality" of language, even if he espoused the idea of the supremacy of a *philosophical* use of language. In any case, a historical study seemed to be called for, but unfortunately, after a few hundred rather uneventful pages, I found that even I was incapable of being persuaded by what I had written.

Both the paltry results of my attempts at history writing and some further thoughts about "invention" ultimately drove me away from my initial historical (or historiographic) concerns and eventually to those inscribed in the second title of the book, *Invention in Interpretation*. These were more contentious, as well as more concerned with the present state of the discourses of the humanities, which increasingly have been determined by the notion that the facts of interpretation are produced by interpretation itself and, thus, in this sense, "invented." Whereas in the first title, "invention" was used rather loosely to mean something close to "beginning," in the second title, it definitely pointed to specific assumptions about interpretation that seem to have a powerful effect on current discussions about interpretation, namely to assumptions about the construed nature of the object of interpretation.

I was primarily reacting against current uses of "invention" (including some contained in my original project) that seem to me to be connected with the rise to respectability of big, sweeping explanations of things whose allegedly construed nature absolves their authors from all concerns with messy beginnings, multiple causes, commensurability, infection, influence, and contact between explanations, and, last, but not least, from any reflection on the status of the explanations produced. Explanation of things through their invention, moreover, also binds the authors who employ it to a degraded Romantic theory of subjecthood that currently translates in the vogue of solemn notions such as "agency" and to an ultimately irrelevant emphasis on "empowerment," as if empowerment could be the result of decisions or policies. When someone suggests to me that something is invented (say, God, matter, or Argentina), I take that person to be implying that that something is after all not the way I thought it was, and also that she is going to tell me how it really is. Then I sadly have to conclude that the switch from hardcore truth by correspondence to warranted assertability has not altered the role of intellectuals in the least. In fact, concerns with invention and devotion to meritorious causes (such as the cause of telling people how things really are) still go hand in hand, and both invariably are paid for by what Wittgenstein used to call a "loss of problems." Versions of invented objects are first and foremost ways of producing self-enclosed, monadic chunks of knowledge that lend themselves admirably to transmission and teaching and that, at the same time, because of their own self-professed nature as discourses about made-up objects, subtract themselves from all possibility of discussion and disagreement. The invented nature of all explanations is a powerful tool for dialectical peace.

This perhaps explains why the consensus in the humanities departments of Western academia about what is teachable (or about what should be taught) never has been so powerful as it is now, when an increasing proportion of what is taught has acquired the status of never-quite-competing ways of worldmaking. Indeed, the incommensurability of versions of putatively invented objects is paradoxically enough the best way of assuring the availability of language and the translatability of all concerns. When one considers their invented nature, they all become indifferent, we all become pluralists, and tolerance becomes the only required virtue. That this is the time in which difference gets *taught* means in this context that this is the time in which difference finally becomes irrelevant, a mere theme among many others.

Because most uses of "invention" in the academy currently are supplemented by explanations about how things were invented, two kinds of implication seem to me to be discernible in principle. The first kind of implication one could call "logical" and relates to hysteron proteron, a phrase that Kant soberly translated as "turning things around." It implies that the predominance of invention brought about revisions in the understanding of predicates such as "being the cause of," "being the consequence of," "being older than," or "being younger than" and perhaps explains the frequent association between invention and metaphors for temporal anomalies, as when one talks about the production of something that was "always already" there.

The second kind of implication I call, for lack of a better word, "intentional." It is twofold. Whenever the status of God, matter, or Argentina is related to invention, intentions are bound to be attributed to a motley class of entities (such as "mankind," "the CIA," "the laws of history," "nature," "the people," "the death drive," and so on) putatively endowed with the power to produce inventions.[6] However, a question also arises as to the plausibility of the status of certain objects said to have been invented as intentional objects— that is, as to the compatibility between the notion that Argentina was invented and the things most people do with their beliefs about Argentina. Such is, in short, the question of knowing whether something that we treat as we treat Argentina (roughly as a complex mess) can be intendable at all.

A popular counterargument (which one could call "the epic theory of invention") suggests that, instead of being the product of scheming little individual minds working in isolation, inventions can be the product of multiple intentions spread over time. However, if one is to retain the unity of the invented product, one is bound to assume that there was at all times a homogeneity of purpose common to all factors relevant to a given invention, and so not only to see Argentina as the result of the spread over time of the intentions of Mr. Jones, Ms. Ramos, the laws of history, and the death drive, but to see it as the product of the *concurrence* in purpose of all these factors.

This kind of explanation seems to me to be unnecessarily sophisticated. Perhaps what most people call God, or matter, or Argentina does not entail any special commitments as to the origin of the thing (fictional or otherwise) and is instead a convenient way to denote a motley set of assumptions and activities that relate to each other in many different ways. If so, there is no way to tell inventions from noninventions, and the whole problem safely can be discarded.

My interests, however, apart from the brief bilious reflections described above (and which will be developed, in a less bellicose mood, in the first section of Chapter 1 below), still had nothing to do with what could be a new sociology of the current uses of "invention" or a futile attempt to argue away the notion of invention as such. The reader should not expect from me therefore any explicit, let alone fully congruent, doctrine of either invention or the meaninglessness of the notion of "invention." Nor did I want to write yet another book on the Western university, a "theory" of invention, or even a theory of things as invented. My interests have rather become both less polemical and empirical in a different sense. Instead of concentrating primarily on my quarrels with the direction that the discussion of interpretation and meaning attribution has taken of late, I have decided to discuss three texts in which, in very different ways, a recognizable claim is made according to which "the facts" (biographical in one case, historical in another, and cognitive in a third) are produced by their own descriptions and interpretations. Each of these three texts, however, also in very different ways and for very different reasons, appears to be incapable of living up to such an ambitious project, less because specific mistakes have been made in the arguments of their authors (I am not even sure all these texts are primarily argumentative) than because the very notion that facts are produced is ultimately unlivable. The form of this latter structure is therefore a problem in interpretation, and has turned this book into something distinct from a motley discussion of interpretations, even if unified by a theme. There is, indeed, a more general claim to it, even if a deceptively simple one, namely that whole collections of infelicities appear to be attached to interpretations that include claims about the unilateral nature of interpretation. And I still am reluctant to commit myself to an alternative theory of interpretation, one that would explain once and for all the cause of such infelicities, nor am I persuaded by the idea that one needs such an alternative theory.

It might very well be that, in the end, the discrepancies between argumentative intention and demonstration prove to be no more than monsters engendered by the sleep of close reading, by the fact that, in what follows, each of these texts has been dealt with primarily in its own terms (a fact that also can account for the quasi-monographic nature of the discussions that follow, as well as for the conspicuous absence of secondary literature, only referred to in footnotes, if at all). I was, as we all were, taught to be wary of phrases such as "dealing with a book in its own terms." And yet, all skepticism notwithstanding, this remains for me a very useful notion whenever I want to describe the shortcomings of what is usually done to books: that is, to express my doubts about the widespread notion that a book essentially is an illustration, or an instance, or a token, of something else. Close reading is one of many possible labels used to describe how one's certainties about what are taken to be the facts of the matter are affected by one's attention to the matter of the facts.

Chapters 2 and 3, dedicated, respectively, to Oscar Wilde's *De Profundis* and Friedrich Nietzsche's *The Birth of Tragedy*, follow inventions gone wrong: Wilde's attempt to invent his own life and Nietzsche's suggestion that one can make up the art of the future. Chapter 4 discusses what I think is still the best, the most intriguing, and the most exasperatingly difficult theory of the roots of invention as such, Kant's *Critique of Pure Reason*, and its relation to the production of both "facts" and knowledge. In a complicated sense it is not about any invention gone wrong, but about Kant's dissatisfaction with, and constant redescription of, the problem of invention.

Oscar Wilde's March 1897 Reading Gaol letter to Lord Douglas has been considered by both its author and its critics as a rare moment of un-Wildean truth and psychological sincerity brought about by personal drama, but I came to realize that the Douglas letter was indeed still part of the Oscar-winning project of making up the facts, namely a person whose *historia calamitatum* and *itinerarium mentis* subsequently were told. Indeed, I now think that everything that Wilde said in "The Decay of Lying" about the Japanese, the nineteenth century, and London fog ("Now, do you really imagine that Japanese people, as they are presented to us in art, have any existence?") applies without restriction to the author of the *De Profundis* letter.

In Chapter 3, several related things that interested me in *The Birth of Tragedy* are discussed. These are things that, for the most part, have been conspicuously absent from the concerns of its numerous and often brilliant commentators. Although Nietzsche's title alludes to a historical problem, the last two-fifths of the book are built around the notion that Greek tragedy will be *reborn*. That detail has led me into investigating Nietzsche's use of the term "rebirth." Oddly enough, "rebirth," understood as a form of improved repetition, also describes rather well what takes place in Nietzsche's own text, because the text we now read was both reborn (in a sense close to Nietzsche's) from previous versions of it and died (if only to resurrect afterward) at the hands of Nietzsche himself in a notorious "Attempt at Self-Criticism" written over a decade later. As any editor of the text has to realize at some point, the latter Nietzsche shows a decided dislike for the notion that the facts about his book have been established once and for all in the first edition and believes that a new interpretation (significantly enough, his own) will not so much get the facts right as, so to speak, redo them. Nietzsche's emphasis on "rebirth" (as well as the correlative emphasis on "birth") is therefore an emphasis on a certain concept of history. According to such a concept, the factual plenum of the past can be reproduced and improved as a correction both to its original version and to some undesirable present, just as one has the possibility of revising manuscripts until they adjust to one's intention.

The interesting thing is that Nietzsche supports this theory in relation to everything but his own manuscript, namely in relation to art, history, and time in general. Wagnerian opera, he believed around the time of the first edition of *The Birth of Tragedy*, would become Greek tragedy reborn, a revised edition, as it were, of its lost original, which had been circulating of late under the debased form of Italian opera. Ever a philologist, he believed therefore in the possibility of resurrecting the past and correcting the present in an improved future. The second part of his book, moreover, is an extraordinary manifesto for a critical edition of pre-Socratic Greece, which he half believed was feasible. There is, therefore, a sense in which, in *The Birth of Tragedy*, time itself, which after Kant had acquired the status of a form of experience and so was independent from all experience, can be turned into an object of experience—that is, can be *used* and, indeed, constructed. One therefore understands why the model of art was so decisive for Nietzsche, and not for purely artistic reasons: it provided him with a description of the general model for the production of facts.

Chapter 4 discusses in detail Kant's hesitations concerning invention in the *Critique of Pure Reason*. The word—let alone the concept—"invention," however, is not an explicit concern of his. Instead, these hesitations are most conspicuously (but not exclusively) expressed in the vocabulary of faculties that he inherited from post-Cartesian philosophy. To the usual list of faculties or powers of the human mind (Reason, Understanding, Sensibility), Kant intermittently considers the possibility of adding the Imagination, the power to create images independent from objects. He is, however, not fully sure of this move. Sometimes the Imagination appears in the first *Critique* as a mere helper to other faculties. In his bolder moments, however, the Imagination acquires an autonomy of its own and becomes the faculty of all faculties, a true metafaculty. In these moments, not only the workings of the Understanding, but also the workings of Reason are described as being literally produced by the Imagination through what Kant terms "figurative syntheses." Such syntheses bind facts to inventions in a double way. First, they synthesize values as specific interpretations of facts, and hence suggest a natural transition between facts and values, rather than a fundamental separation. According to this version, the facts whose description constitutes knowledge proper are interpretively construed—that is, invented—by the Imagination. Second, the Imagination proceeds in a *figurative* way. Accordingly, and very awkwardly, in order for knowledge to be possible at all, it has to remain both figurative and imaginary. Because genuine knowledge for Kant includes both knowledge of the world and knowledge of the knowing subject, both subjects and objects, officially *conditions* for interpretation and knowledge, also are *by-products* of these: that is, invented.

The reader will have noticed that I have omitted Chapter 1 from the summary above. A description of this chapter requires a few additional (and final) remarks. Unlike the other chapters, Chapter 1 is not a monographic essay. Nor is it an essay about what the bulk of the analyses that follow it have in common, let alone a theory of interpretation or invention. In a sense, it tries to capture and develop the traces of the story of this book with which I feel the most reluctant to part, those to which I allude at the beginning of this Introduction. In its first section, the polemical dimension of my concerns is given the shape of a critical analysis of a specific and almost unchallenged contemporary way of doing things with texts, which I call "culturalism." In the second section, I put forth a very general description of the sum of all the different activities known as interpretation. Such is not an a priori description of interpretation, and so it does not appear to merit the usual label of "theory." It is, rather, an ex post facto description of a series of activities for which an a priori description increasingly has appeared to be inadequate, for several reasons. Its mood is theoretical only in the sense that it is "contemplative." In fact, I do not expect these considerations to be capable of being "applied," as "theories," like paint, often are said to be, nor would I know how to apply them myself. And yet I have found them to be useful and have decided to include them in the hope that others might find them of some use, as well.

ONE

Invention and Interpretation

Culturalism

A usual way of suggesting that the study of literature and art deserves to be pursued consists in suggesting that the individual artifacts, apart from features apparent and unapparent such as form and meaning, transcend their individual condition and partake from more general concerns. Words like "civilization," "culture," "class," "society," "human condition," and, of course, "tradition" have been used to refer to these concerns.

A second, also customary, way of explaining how individual artifacts can transcend their individual condition consists in supposing that there is some sort of connection between the features of an artifact and the concerns to which it relates. Different strategies were developed for different features, because the connection between something's being made of stone and its relating to the human condition often is felt to be somewhat different from the connection between something else's saying "I belong to the human condition" and its relating to the human condition. Some of these strategies acquired a specific autonomy of their own, to the point that some people devoted themselves to the construction of vocabularies and to the development of conceptual and descriptive tools meant to deal with features of artifacts and paid very little attention to the connection between the individual artifacts and general concerns. When asked to explain the purpose of their endeavors, they usually talked about the description of things as they really are, or about concentrating on objects for their own sake, or about developing tools that, with proper adjustments, could be used in other fields.

Understandably enough, when dealing with individual artifacts, professionals interested in pronouncements about things in general, as well as in demonstrating the connection between their own activities and things in general, tend to be interested in the transition between the individual artifacts, usually envisaged as a sum of properties, and general terms. Such an interest can explain the otherwise strange principle according to which, for them, individual artifacts primarily serve as examples of general concerns. "Being an example of" is a good example of indicating that there is a connection between two different things. Unfortunately, however, even if you are solely interested in individual features, these also have to be ascribed a certain measure of exemplarity: that is, they also have to be treated as *meaning* something. In any case, whereas the professionals who use words like "civilization," "culture," "class," "society," "human condition," and "tradition" tend to be vulnerable to what Leo Spitzer once called "the toxin of cheap synthesis,"[1] one could say that those who talk about the description of things as they really are tend to be more wary toward big, synthetical pronouncements and explanations.

Literary criticism and the teaching of literature have oscillated between these two positions in the last two hundred years or so. However, the numerous domains and spheres of interest that characterize the activities of critics and professors of literature do not help us to determine a priori the family to which their practitioners belong. There are surprising historians who have refused to in-

tegrate their explanations in a wider doctrine about history, and
there are specialists in prosody who have been firm believers in the
cultural value of certain syllabic patterns, just as there are numerous cases in which this oscillation takes shape within the body of
writings of the same person. Be that as it may, whenever critics
and professors express a *professional* interest for things in general—
that is, an interest for things in general thought to be somewhat
connected to the everyday business of their own profession—they
tend to resent and distrust their peers who do not, those who are
interested in features of artifacts and in less general explanations
and who indeed do not have a theory about the connection between individual artifacts and things in general. For some reason, it
is usually thought that to see the image of the universal in particulars you need to have a "theory," and for a similar reason it is usually thought that intellectuals must be capable of operating irre-
proachable transitions between their professional interests and
their political allegiances. Needless to say, none of these incidents
and divergences has affected the power, political and otherwise, of
intellectuals: in the West, they mercifully always have had none,
perhaps because their condition is not subject to appointment or
sanction by the body politic. One should then perhaps not be too
hasty to see in the recent and rather exuberant proliferation of all-
encompassing claims and critical vocabularies and concerns a mor-
tal threat to literary studies and literature itself. Despite much talk
about culture, gender, ethnicity, difference, race, and class, the
more recent varieties of cultural criticism still belong to the family
of the ultimately moral, if unpretentious, criticism of the likes of
Addison, Johnson, Sainte-Beuve, Emerson, and Arnold (although,
by comparing them with their predecessors, a case could be made
for the decadence of critical prose, dictated—who knows?—by the

prestige of what is considered to be the epistemologically respectable social-science writing style).

This communion is attested by a widespread hostile reaction to a suggestion first put forth by eighteenth-century skeptical philosophy, namely the suggestion that the compatibility between facts (often unproblematically understood by critics as the sum of texts they write about) and values (also often unproblematically understood as the sum of ways in which texts are used), far from having been solved, remains an open question. The question of the relationship between facts and values was indeed crucial to the institutionalization in the university of the teaching of literary analysis. Casting doubts on or even considering the possibility of a problem in such a relationship was always a very minoritary concern of critics. The vast majority of critics instead have chosen to react in many outraged ways to such doubts. One of the most popular of these ways, and certainly one of the most current, consists in supplementing the expressions of moral indignation with hymns dedicated to the various glories of interpretation, among them its alleged property of making up what counts as "the facts": that is, of inventing *values*. It was in this context that invention became a topic closely connected to the topic of interpretation, not least because it increasingly became an a posteriori explanation for the circumvention of the problem of the "facts" of invention themselves—that is, what goes into, on, in, and out of the act of constructing, producing, or making things up.

Doubts as to the compatibility between individual cases and general explanations in the arena of literary studies typically have been put forward by believers in the idea that texts have intrinsic properties. Most such believers, often called "formalists" by their opponents, have tended to rely more or less heavily on the idea of a descriptive language, as well as on the absolute separation between description and explanation, protocol sentences and theory, or, as it was sometimes put in the field of literary studies, poetics and hermeneutics. But then it may be that events in the field of literary studies are but a localized version of a more intricate plot about the contemporary hesitations concerning the idea that objects in general have intrinsic properties.

Most apologies for interpretation, on the other hand, imply the defense of the idea that whatever the intrinsic properties of a text might be thought to be, they are the product of certain specific acts and so are not intrinsic at all. Both "invention" and "interpretation" have been strong candidates in the contest for best general term to describe such specific acts. For antiformalists, the phrase "intrinsic properties" has thus come to denote *pseudo*-intrinsic properties, and terms like "invention" or "interpretation" are considered to denote the *construction* of the kind of properties most people take to be intrinsic. One of the more noticeable consequences of this shift concerns the fact/value distinction, or the lack thereof. Indeed, the word "facts" came to be used as shorthand for the word "values," closely followed by the proviso that no values ever are intrinsic. As Stanley Fish wrote, "fact will be one with value because every thing and action in the world will be seen and engaged with as a manifestation of a controlling aspiration."[2] And values themselves, as this line of argument goes, are historical, constructed and construed—in short, invented. According to a well-known albeit optional postscript to this thesis attributed not altogether unproblematically to Nietzsche, facts are simply values whose construed nature has been forgotten.

It is easy to see that under this sort of conception, interpretations are all there is to know on earth (and indeed all you can possibly know). Less easy to see, and interestingly so, is that this conclusion simply means that all there is to know depends on specific acts of construction on the part of what used to be known as the subject of knowledge. Consequently, this conception of interpretation or of interested meaning-attribution acts coincides with an overly optimistic if not always openly declared theory about universal control by the aforementioned subject. The price of such a control is indicated in the elision of "facts" into "values." What one calls "a text" is therefore simply a set of shared values and beliefs which, of course, are *about* values and beliefs.

Surprisingly enough, just as "formalists" cannot (and sometimes also do not want to) remain mere formalists, so antiformalists seem to be bound to ascribe intrinsic properties, certainly not to texts, but to interpretation itself. For most believers in the constructive virtues of interpretation (that is, for those who believe that *all* interpretations are, even if in a nonderogatory sense, made up), construction itself *cannot* be made up—which is simply to say that it cannot be seen as yet another product of a contingent act of value attribution. Most people can afford to be Nietzschean about the fact/value distinction and talk about the collective illusions of realism. Very few can afford to be openly so concerning values and proclaim that all values are a matter of saying so—that is, a matter of construction and a matter of intention, whichever shape the subject, as the locus of intention, might have. When confronted with the burden of some Humpty-Dumptian theory of meaning, most humanists shy away from it. Humpty Dumpty, be reminded, remarked to Alice that "when *I* use a word . . . it means just what I choose it to mean," and so, for him, "The question is which is to be master."[3]

If I am correct, then, and all appearances notwithstanding, by switching from text talk to interpretation talk one has *not* given up talking about intrinsic properties. The talk about the intrinsic properties of texts simply has been replaced by talk (or by an embarrassed silence) about the intrinsic properties of interpretation. Perhaps, then, the changes in modes of critical discourse described above have been less dramatic than has been generally assumed. Undoubtedly, talking about knowing more about allegedly independent objects such as texts has fallen into disrepute. It is not clear, however, whether talking about the present relevance of certain beliefs is an altogether different activity. In short, there may not be a big difference (although there certainly are many small differences) between saying that a text is a sum of intrinsic properties and saying that a text is really a sum of uses or value-attribution acts. In either case, one is still talking about intrinsic properties, even if in the latter case one is doing so by talking about "having contingent values attributed to it" as an intrinsic property.

Perhaps the supposition of intrinsic properties (of whichever kind) is first and foremost the only way of dealing with texts. I do not mean this in any elegant historicist sense, so I should emphasize that I do not mean "*a* way of dealing with texts." I mean that I know of no *other* way, nor can I even imagine one. In this respect, there seems to be no difference between being a believer in the intrinsic properties of texts and being a believer in the falseness of the belief in intrinsic properties of texts—that is, between being a formalist and being an antiformalist. At this level, antiformalists are right. There is no distinction between facts and values insofar as both these notions are used to denote what one could call the necessary features not so much of an object as of certain actions, of certain dealings with the world.

And yet this does not explain the predominance of antiformalism in the humanities, let alone the brief popularity of formalism itself. In short, it explains neither the concern with the description of mere objects nor the dissatisfaction with such descriptions. What it does help to explain, perhaps, is that apart from short lapses, art criticism, and literary criticism in particular, have been determined by an odd form of dissatisfaction with art and literature themselves. Often, this characteristically has led them into looking for the conditions of their intelligibility in spheres perceived to be higher and more decisive, as it were. The reputation of most such spheres can vary considerably in time and space. "Civilization" and "tradition," for instance, now appear to be dubious terms. "Human condition" has known better days. "Class" and "society" are sometimes perceived to be not universal enough. "Culture," however, at least for the time being, seems to have none of the inconveniences of the others.

There are few notions currently being used in such a generous way as "culture," and not many disciplines as ecumenical as the famed, if nebulous, cultural studies. There, the humanities, the social sciences, and *Populärphilosophie* at last have been reconciled. The very term "culture" is vague enough to be perceived as an equivalent of "civilization" in one or another quarter (if Thomas Mann is still right, the French quarter) and as an equivalent of "society" in some others. Borrowing from Hilary Putnam,[4] one could use the term "culturalism" to describe a set of quasi-consensual albeit complex beliefs and attitudes toward language, art, and literature, and toward the very notion that art and literature have intrinsic properties. Most culturalists tend to believe, for instance, that (1) a text is ("really," as some are wont to add) a set of presuppositions that (2) make it possible for what most people call a text to appear, and therefore believe that (3) things like texts are a posteriori, in the sense that they are the effect of the conditions that cause texts to appear, and so that (4) texts are instances, however indirect, of such conditions. Notions such as "culture," in fact, are used to refer to a set of shared presuppositions that are transcendent *and* transcendental: exterior to and constitutive of certain objects of perception—that is, that are both *not* those objects of perception themselves *and* conditions for those objects to be perceived. Any culture, as culturalists like to say, is not just a context of intelligibility, but also a context of production, in that it constructs the very objects whose intelligibility it subsequently guarantees. Indeed, by appealing to cultural considerations, one simultaneously can displace the problem of intrinsic properties to the realm of interpretation and solve the problem of interpretation itself, displacing it to the consideration of the cultural limits of every interpretation. "Culture" therefore is used to guarantee the absolute empire of interpretation.

Paradoxically enough, "culture" is also used to guarantee the *expendability* of interpretation, in that, since meaning is conceived as intracultural, all problems of meaning already have been solved when one encounters a (produced) object. Production, for culturalists, means therefore the *end* of interpretation: that is, the origin of what is to be interpreted—which, once located, will make the unpleasant regress of interpretation cease. Conversely, the appeal to culture is more often than not the appeal to previously constructed objects, whose properties, in an awkward way, cannot be seen as anything but independent properties. Cultural objects are primarily still-available independent objects whose features have been determined by some unspecified ancestors of ours so as to spare us the uncertainties of meaning-attribution and allow us to use any one of these objects as the automatic token of a preassigned meaning.

In sum, if there is such a thing as a politics of culture, such a politics would be *the* politics of identity, the politics of the operation that converts the use of objects into their one true description. This indeed is what is meant by saying that a culture is a set of values, even when one is prepared to grant the relativistic principle, which always has been self-contradictory and of late also has become common currency, according to which there can be incompatible sets of values and, further, such incompatible sets of values are incommensurable. Indeed, in all these cases, a set of values remains a set of impossible interpretations, which is to say that whenever "culture" gets mentioned, a collection of self-identical objects, withdrawn from all agonies pertaining to meaning-attribution, also gets mentioned in the process.

Interpretive Workout

This analysis of culturalism clearly is an attack on certain anti-formalist accounts of interpretation, but to undertake it is not necessarily to endorse "formalist" theories of interpretation. One could perhaps point out that both appear to be equally caught up in a form of determinism, and that the form of quasi-physical determinism characteristic of formalism differs in this respect little from culturalism's presupposition of a causal link between presuppositions and construed objects. Granted that in most cases presuppositions are seen as contingent and historical, construed objects not only are so, but are perfect, unproblematic illustrations of such presuppositions. If for a formalist the way to end all interpretations is the appeal to interpretation-independent properties, for a culturalist the way to end all interpretations lies in the assumption of a causal contiguity between historical presuppositions and texts. Texts, in this sense, are exemplary because they mean exactly what they are (pre)supposed to mean—no more, no less. Within this metatheoretical preestablished harmony, there is no room for discrepancies between intention and text. At the most, such discrepancies can be left to the account of possible but in principle avoidable dialectic ineptitude, because no one willingly would recognize that a text or an artwork does not after all mean what one *believes* it means. (For example, no one would say, "*Pride and Prejudice* is about incest, but I don't believe it.") Arguments about meaning tend thus to be settled through a process of conversion that need not be dramatic, but that has to dispense with the judicial metaphors usually associated with serious science—that is, with the appeal to interpretation-independent properties.

Another very important consequence of this kind of explanation is a peculiar solution to the venerable Humean puzzle of the derivation of *oughts* from *ises*:[5] that is, the justification for conceiving descriptions of intrinsic properties as yielding behavioral maxims and containing moral injunctions. The problem itself is crucial for those formalists who also are in the business of saving the cultural or moral value of art, because they are bound to know the specific difficulty of relating physical properties to moral evaluations. But since most culturalists appear to be in a parallel line of business, the transition between properties and injunctions also is an important problem for them—although their solution to it is surprisingly simple.

Culturalism just inverts the terms of the problem, deriving what something *is* from how something *ought* to be treated. They can do this because of the assumption that the properties of a text or an artwork are constructed, and that such a construction is made possible by presuppositions. The difference between formalists and culturalists thus again is considerably attenuated here, because in both cases, the practical, moral, aspect of interpretation tends to be the decisive factor. That is, any putative extramoral factors are bound to be either sublated in cultural-value talk (in the formalist case) or seen as consequences of such talk (in the culturalist case). Neither ever can afford to take Hume's famous is/ought "precaution"—that is, give a reason for the derivation of *ought* from *is* (or vice versa), which, if given, as he shrewdly remarked, "would subvert all the vulgar systems of morality." Indeed—and here is a crucial problem of interpretation—there are no appeals to intrinsic properties (although intrinsic properties are a feature of all such appeals), only to interpretations of what counts as being intrinsic. This is just another way of saying that there is no way out of interpretation, if by that one means an intentional way out. And although I will be making much out of the word "intentional" shortly, it seems that as far as things go, culturalists are again right—except for their never being able to be proven wrong.

My own position can be easily summed up. I agree with the culturalists when they imply that things we call "texts" are indeed made-up constructs, in the sense that they are parasitical upon acts of meaning-attribution and in the more trivial sense that texts and artworks do not grow on trees. To their critique, however, I hasten to add that cultural or historical categories, or even alleged human faculties such as invention, although necessary ingredients for their main thesis, seem to be particularly poor cases of it.

This I take as a remark on a curious feature of culturalist arguments: they cannot be wholly culturalist. That is, they don't seem very comfortable with the extreme constructive idea that *everything* is made up. Nor do I think, moreover, that such an impossibility can be overcome, either by a sheer act of will or by an ingenious twist of argument. To be able to overcome it would mean to produce a strange object indeed: an interpretation that would be more than an interpretation—a permanently true interpretation. For some reason, in fact, the idea of interpretation as *mere* interpretation, mere *invention*, is singularly unappealing, even if one can only intend to produce mere (and more) interpretations, as culturalists certainly do. Being more than mere cannot be the result of an act of choice. On the other hand, the very use of argument, if not any use of language, appears to imply (uncomfortably so for culturalists) the impossibility of controlling any culturalist theory along its own lines. This means, among other things, the embarrassing possibility that any intended apology for contingency and history must contain awkward dreams of necessity, even if one does not call them such explicitly.

The reason for this, I think, has in part to do with the kinds of reasons for which, as has been traditionally remarked, relativism or skepticism are self-refuting positions. In a less traditional vocabulary, this might also mean that every act of interpretation, like every act of construction, has to become, at some point, what it cannot even start pretending to be: an awkward claim for some sort of exemption from its own status. Contingency talk, in short, goes wrong, and interpretation can be defined as the unintended going wrong of contingency (that is, the unintended going out of interpretation). Needless to say, this has many implications. The most notorious is that one cannot make up a perfect example of one's own theories, because one cannot completely control their use.

In a roundabout sort of way, we thus arrive here, if not at the question of realism, at least at the question of reality. Perhaps reality could be minimally defined as what happens to an invention. What happens is simply that no invention can work out all the time. We owe the metaphor that describes interpretation as a way of working out things (and a way of making things work out) to Martin Heidegger. In a notorious definition in section 32 of *Sein und Zeit*, Heidegger remarks that "interpretation is not the cognitive acquisition of what is understood but the composition, the working out [*Ausarbeitung*] of the projected possibilities of understanding."[6] Projection, in Heidegger's vocabulary, is the possibility of intentional control of *Ausarbeitung*, the possibility of controlling one's workout (*Ausarbeitung*, I think, is best rendered by translations deprived of all hint of sublimity). In the minimal sense above, reality seems to be therefore equivalent to the episodical not working out of projection. Understood in this way, "reality" could be said to be what the readings that make up this book are about. As long as interpretation is projection (and *all* interpretation cannot help being projection), I would suggest, it *really* cannot work out properly—that is, forever, at all times.

Perhaps this not working out of interpretation as construction is really a not working out of the very idea of working out. I am suggesting that the destiny of interpretation is therefore, and sadly enough, intriguingly parallel to the destiny of other less sublime activities such as self-help, diet, the philosophy of history, and physical workouts: projects and projections can never be anything but imperfect examples of what happens, or, put in a trivial way, you cannot make things happen the way you think. That is why I tried to focus earlier on what is missing in antiformalist and culturalist theories: the agonies pertaining to meaning-attribution, the agonies of invention and interpretation. What happens is never the best possible illustration of an idea about what will happen. Reality I take to be the impossibility of working out such projected possibilities—that is, the difference between interpretation and invention.

Does interpretive workout work out? The answer, in this order, would be "No, and then again yes." The first part of the answer already was implied in the preceding discussion. Interpretive workout does not work out if "working out" is defined as the felicitous invention of the possibilities of understanding and so the a priori description of a conclusion: that is, the production of images of the truth.

But then again, interpretive workout does work out if "working out" is indeed understood as the interference of reality in interpretation. This is perhaps just another way of saying that *in reality* interpretations are possible.

No profession of loyalty to reality or belief in any sort of close encounter with things themselves would help us here, though, since professions of loyalty and narratives of epiphany alike are in this sense still forms of projected intentional control. In my sense, one cannot *be*, let alone become, a realist, but one *cannot help being* one. It is perhaps the case that interpretation works out through the impossibility of projection: that is, through the impossibility of its own intentional control. Working out otherwise would mean being able to dispense with any further interpretation.

To dispense with any further interpretation is a powerful dream, as we saw in the case of culturalism. Nevertheless, a world where interpreting something would be something you do once and for all (e.g., a world in which someone would set out to interpret successfully and permanently *Great Expectations*, the antithetical meaning of primal words, or the end of history) looks rather implausible, except in the classroom. The all-too-obvious conclusion, therefore, is that the workout of interpretation can consist only of its not being able to succeed forever, and so, as has been very often remarked, in its requiring constant corrections. Interpretation works out by being wrong or, better, by one's not being able to help its being wrong. Only apparently is this a lofty and unique case. Indeed, having a discrete temporal span happens every day to yogurt, meat, fish, vegetables, and even to people, about which or whom common wisdom and health departments alike assure us that they are best before a specific date. In more solemn quarters it is called "historicity" or "finitude."

Here is the task for the talks about interpretation that follow: to characterize—alas, with the help of the tools of close reading that were developed by firm believers in the intrinsic properties of texts (the technical legacy of antiformalism is rather dismal)—the impossibility of controlling plots of invention, while, of course, not being able to claim any exemption for it regarding the results of its own task. The title that now belongs to this book uninspiredly calls what affects invention, interpretation, people, and dairy products alike "the matter of the facts."

TWO

Can a Life Be Invented?

"Drudgery, calamity, exasperation, want," Emerson once re-marked, "are instructors in eloquence and wisdom."[1] The point can be taken to imply that calamities and other assorted misfortunes not only have cognitive consequences (and thus a moral use) but, more important, have rhetorical and poetic consequences and belong therefore in the field of language. If one is to follow Emerson's sug-gestion, only in a secondary sense will "calamity" be understood as a theme, because for him, "eloquence" and "wisdom" alike are not necessarily about calamity. Rather, calamity is a constitutive occa-sion for eloquence. Emerson's suggestion is surprising, for, of course, most available theories about calamity presuppose that events and language are different things. In that case, being a realist about ca-lamity would, on the contrary, mean first and foremost that calamity would be treated as a theme (that is, as an entity independent from whatever discourse is employed in referring to it).[2]

Calamity indeed has been treated as a theme since the earliest glosses on the celebrated Peter Abelard's mid-twelfth-century *Historia calamitatum mearum*. Abelard's *Historia calamitatum* is a somewhat autobiographical letter to a friend and the most substan-tial part of a manuscript known as the *Correspondence of Abelard and Heloise.*[3] The text I shall be reading in this chapter, Oscar Wilde's letter to Lord Douglas known both as *De Profundis* and as *Epistola: In carcere et vinculis,*[4] is likewise a somewhat autobiographical letter to a friend. Like Abelard's and Heloise's, it also typically has been understood and valued both as if its narrated events were independent from discourse and had a weight of their own, and also as if they were part of an illustrious tradition. Treating it as the representation of events meant treating the letter as unmediated documentary evidence in the trial of Victorian society that has been playing to large audiences for the past century or so. Treating it as part of a tradition meant establishing all kinds of relationships to other texts, from the Book of Job and Psalm 130 (or Psalm 129), known after the first line of its Latin translation as "De Profundis," to Abelard's *Historia* and Rousseau's or Augustine's *Confessions.*

But even these two seemingly innocuous considerations betray a larger problem. In fact, when held together (as they often are), they imply that *De Profundis* is both about Wilde's life and about a literary tradition. The very reference to the Latin translation of Psalm 130 (or 129) in one of the titles of Wilde's letter constitutes the text of the psalm as a specific "instructor in eloquence" for Wilde's prose. And yet the narrated calamities are supposed to be powerful enough to dispense with any occasions for eloquence other than life itself. The inevitable corollary, which can be read explicitly not only in Emerson's dictum and in most of Wilde's work (except perhaps in his *De Profundis* letter) but in the contemporary critical koine, is not only that what one calls "life" can come down only as language, but especially that life can be instructed only by language—at best, by eloquent language. The events of life therefore are literarily produced—in short, invented. As thematic realism makes a sorry exit, talk about cultural and historical conventions that rule production makes a triumphant entrance.

Tempting as it may be, such a verdict deserves some further scrutiny. A little perhaps could be gained, I argue, from not jumping straight to the jugular of either thematics or conventionalism, and from following Emerson's connection between calamity and persuasive language instead. In this Emerson is not alone. A. Ernout and A. Meillet, in their celebrated *Dictionnaire étymologique de la langue latine* (subtitled *Histoire des mots*),[5] suggest that there is a sense, due "to a connection established in the rustic language between calamus and calamitas,"[6] in which all writing, no matter how persuasive, is calamitous. *Calamus* (like the Greek *kalamos*) means both "shoot" or "straw" and an object made of straw, in particular a writing implement. The linguistic history of this series of metonyms (from straw to object made of straw, from there to writing implement, and thence to calamity) enacts a movement away from a supposedly originary meaning—which, were it not simply too irresistible, could be termed the original lapsus calami, the story of the strange fall of *calamus*, whose semantic argumentum is hard if not impossible for us to apprehend: the story of the straw that broke the writers' back.[7]

My aim in this chapter is even more ambitious. I will proceed from very prosaic writing mistakes in Wilde's text toward the notion that Wilde's text, as perhaps everything we still call literature, is instructed by calamity, and so that even if it is produced, it simply cannot be invented (i.e., produced by someone).

Blots

Toward the end of his *De Profundis* letter, Oscar Wilde makes some remarks concerning the manuscript: "I cannot reconstruct my letter, or rewrite it. You must take it as it stands, blotted in many places with tears, in some with the signs of passion or pain, and make it out as best you can, blots, corrections and all" (230–31).

Whether this passage is an instance of an intended enigma or of a lapse one cannot say. The passage starts as a general statement about the impossibility of rewriting a letter and thus with the definition of "my letter" as "my letter . . . as it stands." There follows a paraphrase of how "it stands." Surprisingly enough, this paraphrase basically amounts to the description of a series of "blots, corrections and all." The enigma, then, or the lapse, derives from the contradiction between the general statement and the paraphrase of the definition: "how it stands" does not conform to the initial description of the object as it is. Indeed, the letter "as it is" amounts, in Wilde's own terms, to no more than a series of reconstructions and rewritings: "blots" and "corrections." Conversely, the mention of a series of reconstructions and rewritings affects, perhaps involuntarily, the earlier general statement. The metaphor of blotting can perhaps be seen thus both as a general description of the effects of *lacrimae in rebus* and as a description of how, in this passage, statements alter statements. Put in another way, Wilde's "tears" are not so much "signs of passion or pain" as what, through some specific form of correction, tears down the sentence "I cannot reconstruct my letter or rewrite it." This I take to be a particular case of what Mark Taylor seems to be saying when he argues that "dif-ference is written 'in' the literary text" in the sense that "the tear of dif-ference is the para inscribed in the praxis of the writer."[8] In fact, "tears" are very real metaphors for the argument in the passage's having gone wrong. Its going wrong means simply that "passion" and "pain" are not so much psychological states that are available for reference, as modes of correction, and so literary procedures. Analogously, Wilde's "make it out as best

you can" is the kind of hermeneutic imperative that appears to describe a very literary predicament, namely the dealing with a torn
text, which in a sense identifies in a rather uncomfortable way what
is mistaken in the interpretation with what is torn in the text interpreted.

The passage, however, seems to proceed in a very different direction:

> As for corrections and errata, I have made them in order that my words
> should be an absolute expression of my thoughts, and err neither
> through surplusage nor through being inadequate. Language requires to
> be tuned, like a violin: and just as too many or too few vibrations in the
> voice of the singer or the trembling of the string will make the note
> false, so too much or too little in the words will spoil the message. As it
> stands, at any rate, my letter has its definite meaning behind every
> phrase. There is in it nothing of rhetoric. (231)

"Corrections and errata" appear to correspond here to the progress
of "absolute expression," of a "definite meaning behind every
phrase," as opposed to the quantitative disturbances of expression
conveyed by the musical metaphors of the violin and the singer.
"Surplusage," as well as "being inadequate," amounts to peculiar disturbances in a quantum ("too many," "too few," "too much," "too
little"), and rhetorical disturbances, at that. Rhetoric seems in fact
to be marked by a peculiar mathematical anomaly whereby meaning
becomes indefinite or rather there is no "exact equivalent" between
"my thoughts" and "my words"—which is to say, there is no "mes-
sage."

Follows a widely known and difficult fable, which deals with the
important tension between this communicational ideal of intentional control of language—in short, of expression—and the history
of its becoming apparent. Understandably enough, Wilde's state-

ment on the subject cannot help being a statement on this particular predicament, indeed the favorite ideal and the worst nightmare of every text editor, namely the inverse proportion acknowledged to exist between the transparency of intention and the number of erasures and substitutions in a given text: "Whenever there is erasion or substitution, however slight, however elaborate, it is because I am seeking to render my real impression, to find for my mood its exact equivalent. Whatever is first in feeling comes away last in form" (ibid.). The condensed chiastic paradox in the latter part of the passage can very well tell the story of the emergence of expression (of the perfect substitution of feeling), and thus the story of the end of impression, the history of form. The earlier part of the passage, however, by focusing on the ingredients of such a process, implies that "real impression . . . comes away last" as errata, as collections of corrections, in which every movement forward is accompanied by the erased inscription of what has been transcended. Rendering implies, therefore, a peculiar exchange whereby form has to give away the traces of its own history, thus telling both the story of "absolute expression" and the way "absolute expression," rather than being the unaltered ingredient or ground of the history of its final triumph, was gradually engendered through "surplusage" and inadequacy— that is, form is rather what "comes away last." The last coming away of form or the temporalized destiny of feeling is thus blotted in through its very history. In this sense, interpretation (or the possibility of unconditioned reversion between form and feeling) is strictly determined by blotting, just as intention cannot help being constantly compared to correction. Indeed, the only possible evidence for "my words . . . err neither through surplusage nor through being inadequate" is the production of "corrections and errata." A consequence among others is then that, in Wilde's own terms, the

best possible equivalent for "there is in [my letter] nothing of rhetoric" is "everything in my letter is rhetoric," since "my letter" was
admittedly written through the disturbances Wilde himself associated with rhetoric (and this point is previous even to any possible
discussion of Wilde's never fully specified yet positively not com-
plimentary definition of the word "rhetoric," or to the notorious usage of hyperbole in a passage against surplusage).

This peculiar status of error is indeed one with the story of the
acquisition of an intentional control over language, as well as with
the misfortunes due to the latter's having to become apparent historically: that is, through a sequence of corrections. Not surprisingly,
errors not usually associated with blots and tears such as what Wilde
calls "psychological error" appear to unwittingly repeat this double
fable of the triumph of intention, to the point that the narrativiza-
tion of "errors" (the core of the so-called psychological novel) can be
shown to be built upon the model of the errata (whose literary correlate might perhaps be the erratic structure of the picaresque down
to *Bouvard et Pécuchet*) and not upon the kind of dialectics of sin
and repentance or ignorance and knowledge most of us would le-
gitimately expect.

Symbol

All the preceding discussion leaves us with an intriguing notion,
according to which "absolute expression," for Wilde, seems to be
the outcome of a series of corrections—that is, that absolute expression is blotted in rather than taken out of life. A more detailed analysis of the figure of "absolute expression" appears therefore to be in
order. Such a figure Wilde often calls, following a firmly established
tradition, symbol. As in most uses of the word, in the wake of Goe-
the and Coleridge, "symbol" denotes what Heidegger called the *Zu-*

sammenbringen, the bringing together of "something other" and the "thing that is made":[9] that is, a peculiar form of "intimacy with which opponents belong to each other [*Innigkeit des Sichzugehörens der Streitenden*]."[10] Wilde's belonging in this family does nevertheless require extensive qualification, and such is the object of the present section.

In a passage whose incipit recalls the title of the third lecture of Heidegger's *Der Ursprung des Kunstwerkes* ("Die Wahrheit und die Kunst" ["Truth and Art"]) Wilde writes:

> Truth in Art is not any correspondence between the essential idea and the accidental existence; it is not the resemblance of shape to shadow, or of the form mirrored in the crystal to the form itself; it is no Echo coming from a hollow hill, any more than it is a silver well of water in the valley that shows the Moon to the Moon and Narcissus to Narcissus. Truth in Art is the unity of a thing with itself: the outward rendered expressive of the inward: the soul made incarnate: the body instinct with spirit. (201)

Two definitions of "truth in art" are sequentially formulated, the first being rejected ("correspondence between" X and Y) and the second being kept ("unity of" X with X). Both definitions correspond to distinctive figures of connection: in the first, words such as "correspondence," "resemblance," "form mirrored," and "Echo" denote a particular operation of synthesis whereby truth is viewed as the result of something's being added on to something else, whether the link between accident and substance or the mimetic connection between "shape" and "shadow"; the second definition, on the other hand, denotes a particular absence of synthesis, in the sense that truth is viewed as derived from nothing's being added on to anything. This second definition begins, indeed, with the figure of the refusal of synthesis (namely pleonasm), gradually giving place to three successive metaphors for this kind of indifference: "rendered expressive of," paraphrased afterwards by two other phrases, "made incarnate" and "instinct with." Both these figures rewrite "expression" in a theological vocabulary (wherein pleonasm becomes strict paradox), by alluding either directly to the Christian incarnation or, less directly, to the Greek *enthousiasmos* via the Ciceronian *instinctus*.[11]

The symbol will be understood by Wilde in this second sense of paradoxical expression. Thus, the general statement "I was a man who stood in symbolic relations to the art and culture of my age" (194), which precedes an extensive list of personal achievements "in the sphere of thought" (ibid.), will ultimately be qualified by the figure that, for Wilde, sums up those achievements—"paradox" (ibid.)—as opposed to precursors such as Byron, who indeed "was a symbolic figure" (ibid.), but whose relations "were to the passion of his age and its weariness of passion" (ibid.). "Mine," adds Wilde, "were to something more noble, more permanent, of more vital issue, of larger scope" (ibid.). And so the symbolic gift ("the gods have given me almost everything," ibid.) translates into a peculiar aptitude for a particular combination of pleonasm and hyperbole, as opposed to any gift for correspondence:

> I made art a philosophy and philosophy an art: I altered the minds of men and the colours of things. . . . I took the drama, the most objective form known to art, and made it as personal a mode of expression as the lyric or sonnet. . . . drama, novel, poem in rhyme, poem in prose, subtle or fantastic dialogue, whatever I touched I made beautiful into a new mode of beauty: to truth itself I gave what is false no less than what is true as its rightful province, and showed that the false and the true are merely forms of intellectual existence. I treated Art as the supreme reality, and life as a mere mode of fiction. . . . I summed up all systems in a phrase, and all existence in an epigram. (Ibid.)

In this particular sense, a symbolic relation can only be indicated through the proliferation of signs of the inadequation between the two poles of "expression" (say "I" and "my age"), through the extensive and hyperbolic indication of the gap which can only be transposed by a god or by someone *entheos*, instinct with, even propelled by calamity. And, of course, the symbolic gift, whose divine origin is explicitly indicated preceding the extensive catalogue above, can only be understood now as a gift to bring together contraries. Indeed, pleonasm and hyperbole alike have something to do with paradox. They both quote definition and synthesis through syntax, as it were (since there are no syntactic differences between analytic and synthetic statements), and also by blowing up predicates to the point that the subject semantically collapses to the inordinate proliferation of its own appendages, no longer subsumable as cognitive achievements.

This particular notion of symbolic relation is thus bound to engender a peculiar form of loss of control over what is brought together, in that the expression of what is brought together necessarily and irrevocably tears apart syntax and semantics, by only allowing the formation of two kinds of expressions: sentences whose truth value can be derived from their syntax (paradoxes and truisms) and blown-up predicates of nonexisting sentences (hyperboles). The fable of this loss is recognized by every reader of the letter in Wilde's personal *historia calamitatum*. However, Wilde himself does not fail to underscore that the thematization of calamities is a metaphor for a previous calamity,[12] which follows and falls from symbolic enthusiasm: "What the paradox was to me in the sphere of thought, perversity became to me in the sphere of passion. Desire, at the end, was a malady, or a madness, or both. . . . I ceased to be Lord over myself. I was no longer the Captain of my Soul, and did not know it. I allowed you to dominate me, and your father to frighten me. I ended in horrible disgrace" (194–95). One can very easily imagine a reading of this passage along the lines of the comparison between "paradox" and "perversity," or even between "sphere of thought" and "sphere of passion," and the way it would almost inevitably emphasize the coincidence between discursive disgrace and ethical and moral disgrace. Such a coincidence, however, is denied from the very start of the passage, namely by the initial opposition between being and becoming, indeed between two distinct temporal states. I quote again: "What the paradox *was* to me in the sphere of thought, perversity *became* to me in the sphere of passion" (my emphasis). In fact, there is nothing originary in perversity, in the trivial enough sense that "perversity" seems to be analogically derived here from "paradox." "Perversity," in this comparison, is rather like a consequence of "paradox." Analogously, the "disgrace" which ends the passage does not close the road opened by the initial reference to the "sphere of passion" (indeed, nothing really "ends": by writing, "I ended in horrible disgrace," the narrator is already placing himself after disgrace); rather, it refers to the loss of the God-given grace of symbolization and so is part of the larger narrative of the adventures of the symbol (and not even necessarily of its final stage). "I ceased to be Lord over myself" was then referring to "paradox" before it became attached to "perversion."[13] Along that narrative, "symbol" refers to two different situations, as it refers to two distinct temporal states: the symbol that "I was," no longer intact, and the symbol as revealed through a *historia calamitatum* (what the symbol has become), which converts the description of past states of affairs into the sign of a "horrible disgrace" that will fabricate itself. In any case, the past becomes adequate to the present only through its difference in relation to the present, acquiring a different degree of intelligibility through the consideration of its own history, of what it has become. "I was a man who stood in symbolic relations to the art and culture of my age" is then both the description of a past moment and the description of a past moment as a lost moment. The discontinuity between past and present confers to intelligibility an anachronic status: only by means of the retrospective narrative of its loss can any sense of adequacy be restored.

For the structure of the symbol, the temporal discontinuity will translate into a temporalized sense of expression which corresponds to a deferral introduced by history. The notion of expression will be redefined along these lines later in the letter, during a discussion of the Messiah as foreseen in a prophecy of Isaiah:

> Every single work of art is the fulfillment of a prophecy: for every work of art is the conversion of an idea into an image. Every single human being should be the fulfillment of a prophecy. For every human being should be the realisation of some ideal, either in the mind of God or in the mind of man. Christ found the type, and fixed it, and the dream of a Virgilian poet, either at Jerusalem or at Babylon, became in the long progress of the centuries incarnate in him for whom the world was waiting. "His visage was marred more than any man's, and his form was more than the sons of men," are among the signs noted by Isaiah as distinguishing the new ideal, and as soon as Art understood what was meant it opened like a flower at the presence of one in whom truth in Art was set forth as it has never been before. For is not truth in Art, as I have said, "that in which the outward is expressive of the inward; in which the soul is made flesh and the body instinct with spirit: in which form reveals"? (800)

The most important feature of such a redefinition is introduced through the comparison between "conversion of an idea into an image" and "fulfillment of a prophecy." Such a comparison implies an important change in the temporality of conversion itself, as indeed it does imply a major change in the theology of incarnation. The change corresponds to the introduction of a temporal prerequisite, so to speak, in whose terms what is to be converted (i.e., what is to be attributed meaning) can only be so after a period of waiting. Analogously, incarnation (leaving for the moment the fact of being poetically constructed) can take place only after a "long progress of centuries." Prophecy corresponds thus to an unrealized ideal, as symbolic adequation is deferred on to the future. However, the deferral of the apocalyptic moment, the moment of the revelation of meaning, renders the sensible manifestation of the symbol unrecognizable as such. The quote from Isaiah (52:14) mentions a disfigured Messiah, aesthetically irrelevant as to His meaning. This disfigured Messiah functions thus as a double emblem: on the one hand it stands for the very calamity of adequation brought on by history; on the other hand it stands for the unrecognizability of what is to be symbolized. The "body . . . in which Form reveals" is then compared, through Isaiah, to a deformed body ("his form was more than the sons of men"), just as truth in art (expression, incarnation, or enthusiasm) becomes determined by the gap between language and reference, between the manifestation of the symbol and what the symbol is about.

In Wilde's letter, one of the recurrent compositional ways of dealing with this duplicity of the symbol is precisely the presupposition of an unconditioned identity between the story of the *I*'s current misfortunes and "the four prose-poems about Christ" (211) via the analogy established between the Scriptures and Greece, the Greek language, and the Greeks (namely Plato, Sophocles, and Euripides), which provides the basic context of intelligibility to the *historia calamitatum*. Two theses support the analogy. The first is both a historical and a literary thesis, according to which Christ is "the precursor of the Romantic movement in life" (213) and "Shelley and Sophocles are of his company" (205); no wonder, then, that "the ultimate survival of the Greek Chorus, lost elsewhere to art, is to be found in the servitor answering the priest at Mass" (206). In its terms, the historical narrative builds up a temporal continuity (and ultimately a synchrony) between three distinct temporal states (the present, the Greek past, and the Romantic past). The second thesis is a linguistic thesis, according to which "it is extremely probable that we have the actual terms, the ipsissima verba used by Christ . . . [since] now we know that the Galilean peasants, like the Irish peasants of our own day, were bilingual, and that Greek was the ordinary language of intercourse all over Palestine, as indeed all over the Eastern world" (211–12):

> I never liked the idea that we knew of Christ's own words only through a translation of a translation. It is a delight to me to think that as far as his conversation was concerned, Charmides might have listened to him, and Socrates reasoned with him, and Plato understood him: that he really said *ego eimi ho poimen ho kalos*: that when he thought of the lilies of the field, and how they neither toil nor spin, his absolute expression was *katamathete ta krina tou agrou pos auksanei. ou kopia oude nethei*, and that his last word when he cried out "My life has been completed, has reached its fulfilment, has been perfected," was exactly as St. John tells us it was: *tetelestai*: no more. (212)

Translations of translations, in fact, do not grant any special cognitive privileges as to what Wilde calls here, once more, "absolute expression." Conversely, epistemological reliability is achieved through a common language whereby all semantic and intentional puzzles are a priori solved. The conversation of mankind can take place only in a lingua franca. To the disliked idea of a "translation of a translation" Wilde opposes here the description of a presumably delightful conversation. In such a conversation all historical distance between precursors has been suppressed (commonness of language being able to make up for temporal discontinuity) and, most of all, the *I* (i.e., a metaphor for the "Irish peasants" above) can take part in it not just by occupying a place in the chain of intelligibility thus pictured (most likely above Charmides), but also by effectively suppressing the historical distance between the precursors and himself, by suppressing the waiting of the prophecy of which he is the sensory, the aesthetic, fulfillment. Only by being what is announced by his precursors, by being their interpretant, can the *I* use adverbs like "really" and "exactly" to qualify words attributed to them and so restore the suppressed history in the synchronicity of an incarnated symbol.[14]

Such a synchronicity, one might say, is typically built through a double operation: in a first stage, waiting is suppressed through an ellipsis of the temporal lapse between meaning and manifestation; in a second stage, meaning is unconditionally metaphorized in manifestation. These two operations correspond to the double movement of suppression and restoring of history through which symbols acquire their power. Unfortunately, they also correspond to the very duplicity of the symbol, in that they tend to lead to a process of symbolic degradation whereby the difference between past and present is reinstated through a deliberate disfigurement of the present. This amounts to saying that, even if an alleged commonness of reference and sign allows for the symbolizing nature of the present, the apocalyptic moment of the appearance is indicated by numerous traces of default rather than by the ultimate fulfillment of a past, and that the symbol emerges to the senses as a parody of its very meaning:

> Everything about my tragedy has been hideous, mean, repellent, lacking in style. Our very dress makes us grotesques. We are the zanies of sor-

row. We are clowns whose hearts are broken. We are specially designed to appeal to the sense of humour. On November 13th 1895 I was brought down here from London. From two o'clock till half-past two on that day I had to stand on the centre platform of Clapham Junction in convict-dress and handcuffed, for the world to look at. I had been taken out of the Hospital Ward without a moment's notice being given to me. Of all possible objects I was the most grotesque. When people saw me they laughed. Each train as it came up swelled the audience. Nothing could exceed their amusement. That was of course before they knew who I was. As soon as they had been informed, they laughed still more. For half an hour I stood there in the grey November rain surrounded by a jeering mob. (219)

The narrative of this particular transit ("John 19:1–5 in Clapham Junction" would be an apt title for it) is preceded by literary considerations by the narrator which unanimously emphasize the displacement that has taken place. The "tragedy" of the symbol is "lacking in style" as the possibility of a delightful conversation with the precursor narrative converts itself into an actual narrative event and the timeless occasion of the colloquium with Socrates and Christ becomes "November 13th 1895." The pathos of the Passion has accordingly been altered as the first-person narrative comes to denote a subject marked by the disproportion between his immoderate wish for tragedy and his innate talent for the unintentional grotesque, "specially designed to appeal to the sense of humour." Not only has this subject, for lack of available evangelist, to write about himself *d'outre tombe* ("I was brought down here from London"), as the first-person narrative by no means denotes any kind of acquired power ("we are clowns whose hearts are broken"), let alone the sort of protagonism we persist in associating with subjecthood. One has instead a grammatical subject referred to through passive constructions ("I was brought down," "I had to stand," "I had been taken out," even "I stood there") and compared to an object, "of all possible objects . . . the most grotesque." In fact, the symbol, whose ideal meaning might very well have been tragic, becomes sensory as a farce. One would almost like to add that the symbol of an age is necessarily "repellent," at least from the point of view of the one who witnesses the conversion of the stations of the Cross into railroad stations as his own poetic intentions become apparent only through a lack of style. One would have then to take very literally what Wilde himself wrote in a particularly prophetic (and thus unintentional) moment: "the little things of life are symbols" (183).

Sorrow

The discussion of Wilde's use of "symbol" has gradually taken us away from what is safely presumed to be known about the so-called Symbolist movement to the analysis of a peculiar difficulty. Such is, at bottom, a difficulty of what Wilde often calls truth—that is, a difficulty of adequation. Nowhere is such a difficulty so apparent as in Wilde's considerations about the very becoming of symbol (and "becoming" can mean here both destiny and adequation to a past, almost in the sense of decorum). Indeed, the fulfillment of symbols is typically deferred on to a future, when such a fulfillment will become inadequate: that is, when what will become will not be becoming.

Seen retrospectively, then, past events contain an ambiguous promise, a proclamation of both manifestation and disaster made in the mode of necessity, apparent in what Wilde calls "the note of Doom that like a purple thread runs through" (204) the texture of several of his works.[15] So, he writes, there is a future "foreshadowed and prefigured in my art" (203), the relation between proclamation and meaning being irrelevant, and pointing to such a mode of necessity. Prefiguration can be read retrospectively as the overcoming of a past state of unawareness ("a phrase which when I wrote it seemed to me little more than a phrase," 204), the result of a deliberate and overt poetic act (such as the construction of "recurring motifs," ibid.), the product of an act of occultation (something "hidden away," ibid.) or of a deliberate act of proclamation (something "set forth in many colours," ibid.). The multiplicity of cases, as well as the multiplicity of hermeneutics they would require, denotes rather the expression of an "it could not have been otherwise" (ibid.), of a general symbolic law: "at every single moment of one's life one is what is going to be no less than what one has been. Art is a symbol because man is a symbol" (ibid.). According to that law, each and every moment is both the figure of a past and the announcement of a figure: that is, both the fulfillment of a presumably past "note of Doom" and the announcement of yet more "Doom." And so the unity of the symbol tends to be more akin to a common inevitability of becoming than to an identity in substance between what is shown and what shows. Here is how a passage amply discussed in the preceding section, the passage where indeed one can read the supremacy of the symbol as a mode of contiguity as well as its demise, continues:

> Truth in Art is the unity of a thing with itself: the outward rendered expressive of the inward: the soul made incarnate: the body instinct with spirit. For this reason there is no truth comparable to Sorrow. There are times where Sorrow seems to me to be the only truth. Other things may be illusions of the eye or the appetite, made to blind the one and cloy the other, but out of Sorrow have the worlds been built, and at the birth of a child or a star there is pain. (201–2)

The word "Sorrow" had occurred earlier in the paragraph ("behind Sorrow there is always Sorrow. Pain, unlike Pleasure, wears no mask," 201), as an emblem of the kind of perfect adequacy (i.e., "unity," as opposed to "correspondence" or, as we have seen, "translation") associated elsewhere by Wilde with the standard post-Romantic doctrine of symbol (if there is such a thing). According to such a doctrine, in "there is no truth comparable to Sorrow" "Sorrow" has to be read as a hyperbolic example of truth and as the ultimate case of "unity of a thing with itself." The sentence has therefore to be read as an elliptic form of "there is no truth comparable to the truth of Sorrow," and sorrow (or "pain") becomes the transcendent metrum of cosmic rhythm alluded to by the very last part of the passage.

In that same sentence, however, "Sorrow" seems to designate something else, namely an immanent principle of generation ("out of Sorrow have the worlds been built") and so, in the genealogy thus established, the prefiguration of "the worlds." "At the birth of a child or a star there is pain" would then have to be read as both a hysteron proteron and an anastrophe of "there is pain at the birth of a child or a star."[16] In this sense, truth, "the outward rendered expressive of the inward: the soul made incarnate: the body instinct with spirit," is what is built out of sorrow, the sorrow of truth being both its origin and the fact that, in a second sense, "there is no truth comparable to Sorrow"—that is, that truth is itself a symbol, and a sorry one at that, of sorrow. In this latter sense, "there is no truth comparable to Sorrow" would be a hyperbolic characterization of "sorrow" (e.g., literally, "Sorrow is incomparable") as well as a derogatory characterization of "truth" as mere truth. This latter interpretation is reinforced by the sentence that immediately follows the general formula ("There are times where Sorrow seems to me to be the only truth"), where truth is described as being perceived (at times) as a form of sorrow. "The unity of the thing with itself" (as well as the nostalgia of perfect adequacy) is thus produced by sorrow, and is a symptom of the inadequacy between what shows and what is shown.

The celebrated end of the letter describes this peculiar concept of truth as connected to a peculiar teaching and learning practice, in this case enacted in the relationship between the author of the letter and "dear Bosie": "You came to me to learn the Pleasure of Life and the Pleasure of Art. Perhaps I am chosen to teach you something much more wonderful, the meaning of Sorrow, and its beauty" (240).[17]

This seems to be a passage where a particular teaching situation is described (the situation of what Wilde, two lines above, calls a "terrible school"), namely through the supposition of hierarchical levels marked by the disproportion between *you* (the student) and *I* (the teacher). Such levels quote the peculiar symbolic temporal syncretism of the colloquium between Christ and Socrates (and the "chosen" *I*, of course), on the one hand, and disciples in general, Charmides and *you*, on the other, in which is marked the innate superiority of teachers over students.

The passage nevertheless is far from describing a teaching situation along the lines of a clear-cut meaning-transmission situation, either one in which the expectations of the student are met by what is actually taught and thus in which the student controls, through anticipation, the contents of teaching, or one in which the teacher determines what is actually taught. In fact, meaning-transmission is the whole problem, as the passage is established over the misunderstanding that constitutes teaching (moreover defined as the teaching of "the meaning" of something): that is, the very transcendence of meaning itself. The difference between the two levels is in fact signified not as a difference in knowledge so much as a difference in the control of knowledge, whereby both the unsuccessfulness of the intention of the *you* and the irrelevance of the intention of the *I* are what define what gets taught. The expression "much more wonderful," then, denotes both a misapprehension of what the teacher considers he has taught and the full disproportion between teacher and student that constituted the teaching situation in the first place. In the terms of the latter, then, the *you* gets taught through the choosing of the wrong teacher, as what is taught is considered to be other than what had been anticipated by the student, and the teacher teaches because he has been "chosen" (and not by the student) to do so. Just as the *you* had been defined from the outset as "merely a puppet worked by some secret and unseen hand" (172), to whose activities correspond, in the terms of the symbolic lyceum alluded to above, the "listening" of Charmides and the "understanding" of Plato (212), so does the teacher express some doubts ("perhaps," 240) as to his own autonomous protagonism: "to be entirely free, and at the same time entirely dominated by law, is the eternal paradox of human life that we realise at every moment; and this, I often think, is the only explanation possible of your nature, if indeed for the profound and terrible mystery of a human soul there is any explanation at all, except one that makes the mystery more marvellous still" (172).

"The meaning of Sorrow" (240), then, is inseparable from the very gap lying at the heart of the ipsissima verba of the teaching situation, which is to say, inseparable from the strict impossibility of the kind of division of labor implied by the symbolic model of the colloquium: "Sorrow" means both that one does not get taught what one expects to get taught and that the putative superiority of those who teach the unexpected does not translate into any sort of autonomy of the teacher. The meaning of sorrow resembles thus more the teacher's description of a discordant lament of student and teacher over the shortcomings of language, over what Italo Svevo once called *la stupida lingua*, as well as the inadequacy between the meaning of teaching and its very figure, as expressed by the disgruntled teacher's discourse.

So one should take somewhat soberly the teacher's peroration ("incomplete, imperfect, as I am, yet from me you may have still much to gain," 239–40), namely for its rather unparadoxical face value and beyond the misleading "yet." The first part of the sentence appears in this light to be less a tribute to modesty than the logical antecedent of the second part. It is precisely because I am incomplete and imperfect that you haven't gained all that you can gain yet. But, of course, since I am and presumably will remain "incomplete" and "imperfect," I cannot vouch for any future gains either. So the "hope that our [future] meeting will be what a meeting between you and me should be, after everything that has occurred" (238) is indeed a hope for a symbolic (and involuntary) repetition of a past, for the impossible symbolic adequacy between master and disciple: what "should be" is, as always, what we "are," and, from that perspective, nothing has occurred, if by that one is implying that the student has acquired something and the teacher has managed to have the student acquire something: "In old days there was always a wide chasm between us, the chasm of achieved Art and acquired culture: there is a still wider chasm between us now, the chasm of Sorrow: but to Humility there is nothing that is impossible, and to Love all things are easy" (ibid.). This passage is preceded by the expression of the hope quoted above and indeed can be understood both as the prescription of a future attitude to a notoriously incompetent replacement for Charmides in the vocabulary traditionally attributed to one of the symbolic replacements of Socrates (i.e.,

Christ)—"Humility" and "Love"—and the verification that nothing has indeed occurred: "In old days there was . . . a wide chasm between us," "there is a still wider chasm . . . now." In the terms of the former prescription, "Humility" and "Love" are the processes through which the past is transcended,[18] and sorrow, no longer incommensurable, is attributed a meaning. In the terms of the latter verification, however, all images of transcendence are out of place, since "a wide chasm" can only be replaced by "a still wider chasm." Conversely, the verification announces the likely prospect of any attempt at meaning-attribution and hence the impossibility of interpretation and the failure of imagination as an autonomous faculty.[19]

Far from being a self-reflecting description of the *I*, "Sorrow" seems to be used rather as a concept, or at least as a designation for a motley set of dialectical maneuvers which in a way denote a major complication in meaning-attribution procedures, namely that the possibility of meaning-attribution cannot be distinguished from its empirical results and so from specific accounts of failed meaning-attributions. There is thus a very important sense in which Wilde's letter itself has to become the destiny of symbol, and so a sense in which this process can only take place in language—the language of the letter as we have it.

The process is not unlike what takes place in the restoring of the full text of the letter, as textual criticism is indeed a privileged emblem of the restoration of a totality through the supposition of previous arbitrary elisions and cuts, intentional or otherwise. So it is only fitting that the restored paragraph where the first, truncated, edition begins (the first edition had omitted what in the Hart-Davis edition are now the first thirty-three pages of the text) would have added four lines which uncannily point to the necessity of chasm, followed, after the brief transition of a mere "but," by an apology for contiguity: "All this took place in the early part of November of the year before last. A great river of life flows between you and a date so distant. Hardly, if at all, can you see across so wide a waste. But to me it seems to have occurred, I will not say yesterday, but to-day" (186). In fact, "but," referred afterwards to the *I* in a weakened mode ("to me it seems"), is the only sign of the operation which converts "November before last" and "a date so distant" into "to-day," and so of the operation of transcending the "great river of life" by inscribing this metaphor in the coincidence between "yesterday" and "to-day." In consequence, "Hardly, if at all, can you see across so wide a waste" is offered two incompatible interpretations in a rapid succession, in the terms of the first of which the past is irrevocably cut in its intelligibility from the present, and in the terms of the second of which such a condition is revoked. Every reader of the letter in the Hart-Davis edition will have noticed that the first thirty-three pages correspond to literary procedures that were omitted from the first edition, namely lengthy and painstaking descriptions of unrepeatable circumstances and their regalia: proper names, prices, and actions (which of course are also expurgated by the first editor from all subsequent paragraphs).[20]

So, just as when the second text in the transition to the first text works out a transition between "yesterday" and "to-day," so the first text begins as inscribed in the second text in the mode of timeless totality, from which will be erased all descriptions of "yesterday":

> Suffering is one long moment. We cannot divide it by seasons. We can only record its moods, and chronicle their return. With us time itself does not progress. It revolves. It seems a circle round one centre of pain. The paralysing immobility of a life, every circumstance of which is regulated after an unchangeable pattern, so that we eat and drink and walk and lie down and pray, or kneel at least for prayer, according to the inflexible laws of an iron formula: this immobile quality, that makes

each dreadful day in the very minutest detail like its brother, seems to communicate itself to those external forces the very essence of whose existence is ceaseless change. (Ibid.)

The topic of this gloss on the "long moment" of "suffering" (that Wilde shortly afterwards will call "the season of Sorrow") is the exclusion of every temporal correlative of difference. Division ("we cannot divide it") is replaced by recorded "moods"; progress ("time itself does not progress") is replaced by several geometrical metaphors (such as the movement of revolution and the "circle round one centre of pain"), as well as by "paralysing immobility"; and "ceaseless change" is replaced by an "immobile quality." Analogously "the inflexible laws of an iron formula" seem to be directed against any possibility of chasm, temporal or otherwise. These laws presumably determine a principle of temporal replication ("each dreadful day in the very minutest detail like its brother") which converts the day (metonymically signified by the minute description of a reiterated *emploi du temps*) into the unit of the return, so that each day returns next day. Indeed, they determine a principle of replacement that "communicates" to "external forces" the attributes of the day so defined and therefore, in spite of the pronounced signs of aversion of the *I* as well as of his skeptical posture,[21] extends his authority to every possible object of description.

No great wonder, then, that the following paragraph will carefully work out a transition between time so conceived and writing: "In the sphere of thought, no less than in the sphere of time, motion is no more. The thing that you personally have long ago forgotten, or can easily forget, is happening to me now, and will happen to me again to-morrow. Remember this, and you will be able to understand a little of why I am writing to you, and in this manner writing" (ibid.). The transition between "sphere of time" and "sphere of thought" is simultaneously guaranteed and weakened by the fact that the passage itself is referring to the writing of the passage (to the point that organizing a transition is already "in this manner writing" such a transition). "Motion is no more," then, both proleptically refers to a manner of writing (it announces a style, so to speak, wherefrom all references to temporal chasms have been deleted) and is produced as a topos by a manner of writing. Such a manner is, first and foremost, a manner of control envisaged as a control over time.[22] The *you* and the *I* are divided along the lines of their anamnestic capabilities, and the *I* assumes not so much the control of memory (not perhaps unlike the holder of the teaching position discussed above) as he does the position of necessary *terminus ad quem* of all events("[this] is happening to me now, and will happen to me again to-morrow"), not unlike the personification of a classic. The final injunction ("Remember this") is thus quite close to a ghostly "Remember me": only by remembering that I can remember what you forgot (as I literally become what you forgot) will you "be able to understand a little of why I am writing to you, and in this manner writing." Only classics (such as Oscar Wilde and Hamlet's defunct father) can in this strict sense be understood: how little so is what both *Hamlet* and what follows show, albeit in very different ways.

What follows is a paragraph (kept in all editions of the work) containing a procession of signs of "yesterday." The paragraph appropriately narrates, from "here," the story of Wilde's mother's death (in the sequence of the strict Hamletian analogy of the preceding paragraphs), enmeshed in a series of temporal and spatial locutions ("a week later," "three more months," "then," "Genoa," "England") which reintroduce the kind of temporal caesuras whose irrelevance had been one of the main targets of the preceding paragraph. As could be expected, this yesterdaylike event is also incompatible with the poetic rules laid down immediately before, as no "in this manner writing" seems to adjust to "the purple pageant of my incommunicable woe" (ibid.): "Her death was so terrible to me that I, once a lord of language, have no words in which to express my anguish and my shame. Never even in the most perfect days of my development as an artist, could I have had words fit to bear so august a burden. . . . What I suffered then, and still suffer, is not for pen to write or paper to record" (ibid.).

"No words for terrible events," of course, is a consecrated topos. Such a topos, however, is reconverted here as it becomes integrated in the full history of symbolic inadequacy. Just as it has been considered, through the supposition of a law of symbolic consequences, that "the most perfect days of my development as an artist" were ultimately symbolized by a "horrible disgrace" (195), through which "I, once a lord of language" (186), "ceased to be Lord over myself" (195), so the literary consequence of a former "disgrace" (the "in this manner writing") does not represent any overcoming of past poetic inadequacies, as it is unfit "to bear so august a burden." In fact, "not for pen to write or paper to record" works simultaneously as the symbolic ideal, as well as the consecrated topos, of sorrow and as a never-to-take-place consequence of sorrow. "In this manner writing," by becoming the only possible consequence of the "No words for terrible events" topos, is thus synonymous with the empirical degradation of the topos, with the sorry following of a topical rule, which parallels the general form of degradation of the symbol through which what becomes is by necessity never becoming. Thus there seems to be an important divergence between the preestablished symbolic telos of the figure of adequacy (which would lead to annihilation and to the impossible discourse of "incommunicable woe") and the way in which such a telos is annihilated through a series of imperfect and inadequate appearances. The latter in a sense determine the precedence of language over prospective imagination, as they do establish what one could call the necessary inadequacy of "writing": in a certain sense, not even "no words" is becoming to sorrow, as "sorrow" itself designates not an operation of a faculty (say, imagination) but only what comes down as discourse.[23] The rescuing of the description of psychological states by language has notwithstanding to be considered as yet another unintended offense directed against the faculties of the soul.

Nor indeed does history so described lead into any *Aufhebung*, even if momentary, contained in the notion, however catastrophic, of "in this manner writing." In fact, the refusal to acknowledge seasons and movement, and the related formulation of history as a nauseous form of eternal recurrence, do not correspond to any sort of emancipation of the present from the past, as "in this manner writing" is an uncontrollable program, at least as uncontrollable as the "this" in the expression. In fact, it can mean both the ideal of the suppression of every temporal chasm and its unfortunate symbolizing in the proliferation of instances of temporal caesuras, often by the working out of quasi-imperceptible transitions that, by rendering possible the reference to "yesterday," assert the essential difference between "yesterday" and "to-day," as in what follows: "Three more months go over. The calendar of my daily conduct and labour that hangs on the outside of my cell-door, with my name and sentence written upon it, tells me that it is Maytime" (187). The first sentence, while obviously belonging to the family of the second meaning of "in this manner writing," does not belong to the first one, since it is incompatible with the previous description "motion is no more" (186). The second, longer, sentence, nevertheless, enacts the transition that will culminate in the first sentence (hysteron proteron being here again the dominant figure). It starts with a reference to "the calendar of my daily conduct and labour" (187), in itself a metaphor of past metonymical descriptions of a daily schedule, and thus redescribes what was termed earlier as "the paralysing immobility of a life every circumstance of which is regulated after an unchangeable pattern" (186). The calendar is, however, "written upon" (187), and this late addition of writing is what allows for the transition to start to develop. In fact, the modification introduced in the description of a recurring schedule consists in the introduction of two factors of contingency, "my name and sentence" (ibid.), which announce what was defined as sorrow as a seasonal event and by no means the substance of the only season. The initial metaphor for recurrence is thus aptly disturbed by the emergence of something "written upon," which indicates, through two different kinds of restriction, that at any rate, in "For us there is only one season" (186), "for us" remains the decisive element. The first restriction reduces the plural-*majestatis* to a contingent *I* (to which corresponds, presumably, a proper name), as the second restriction, the temporal determination of the "sentence," defines a scansion in time and therefore a plurality of seasons. The modification introduced by writing is inherited by the final prosopopoeia ("The calendar . . . tells me that it is Maytime"), not so much in any logical sense (since the only law here is the law of mere neighborhood) as in that the attribution to a calendar of a "seasoned," *scanded*, discourse contrasts to its schedular implications in a way that parallels the effects of writing on the calendar.

From the statement attributed to the calendar ("It's Maytime") to the initial statement by the narrator ("Three months go over"), on the contrary, there seems to be a relation of inference ("If it is May, then three months must have gone over since X"), which ultimately, and beyond all the considerations on eternal recurrence, brings us back to the "yesterday" of "the early part of November of the year before last" (186). This description, in spite of the promises contained in the "in this manner writing" of the same paragraph, will be complemented by next paragraph's "a week later" and "three months go over," enabling us to reconstruct a detailed chronology—that is, to scand the time between "November" and "May" in at least four different "seasons": one in which "all this [whatever it may have been] took place" ("the early part of November of the year before last"), one in which "I am transferred here" ("a week later," ibid.), one in which "my mother dies" ("three more months go over and . . . ," ibid.), and one in which "the calendar . . . tells me it is Maytime" ("three more months go over," 187).

A general problem seems thus to be gradually arising, namely the problem of the relation between the complex structure Wilde calls "Sorrow" and the very shape of the letter. That problem brings us back to the notion of *historia calamitatum*, or, rather, to the connection between the two words in this expression. I remarked at the outset that calamity is mostly considered to be a theme. For critics, this means that, like all themes (but the same could be said about genres), it is considered to be a separate, a priori, entity, available in principle to endless linguistic replications. Inasmuch as it gives this kind of status to thematic considerations, criticism is always bound to be a minor species of realism *sans le savoir*, vulnerable to all variety of embarrassments. ("Why are there plenty of literary ideas of 'sorrow' or 'love,' whereas literary ideas of 'chair' are so scarce?") The standard antirealist answer, however, is hardly satisfactory, either. Considering calamities and sorrow to be products and inventions, conventions affected by historical contingencies and created by language, is still a form of idealism whose self-professed infatuation with the idea of materiality is, at best, a defense mechanism and, at worst, genuine. From Emerson, I have taken a preliminary suggestion that got us away from the polarity of themes and conventions which seemed to be destined to infect this kind of discussion, namely the notion that there appears to be a relation between calamity and persuasive language. Wilde's letter, I take as yet another answer. According to that answer we could perhaps call calamity a specific event: the fable of the difficulty of controlling a mere product, in the sense of actually saying what you mean—that is, the fable of what happens to you when you use language. The first section of this chapter points to a well-known root of such difficulty, namely that meaning something is always correcting something (hence the blots). Reading a series of corrections is therefore, in my sense, reading a *historia calamitatum*. Given, however, that, like every other reading, my reading, as has been unfortunately made obvious, is itself too much like Wilde's—that is, is "blotted in many places"—I have been, indeed, and unwittingly, writing a *historia calamitatum mearum*. Both stories are therefore products which no sum of human beings or historical circumstances (let alone I myself) could possibly have meant.

THREE

Can Art Be Made?

One cannot blame readers for approaching the latter part of Friedrich Nietzsche's first published book, *The Birth of Tragedy*,[1] with wary minds. Whereas the first fifteen sections of the book correspond rather obviously to its title, the last ten deal with what Nietzsche terms the "Wiedergeburt der Tragödie," the "rebirth of tragedy." Accordingly, the first three fifths of the book have been valued at the expense of the last two fifths.[2] This latter part has been sometimes perhaps too emphatically identified with a verbose apology for Wagnerian opera. Those who subscribe to this tradition of commentary can claim on their behalf the corroboration of no less an authority than Nietzsche himself. However, in what follows my contention will be that there is more at stake than a mere preference for Wagner (or, later, Bizet) on Nietzsche's part. Indeed, to believe that one can bring about the rebirth of anything is to believe in a certain way that the future can be produced. The outcome of such belief in *The Birth of Tragedy* is the focus of this chapter.

In his famously caustic and also very oblique "Versuch einer Selbstkritik" ("Attempt at a Self-criticism"), printed as a preface to the third edition of the work (1886), Nietzsche complained bitterly about having "spoiled the grandiose Greek problem . . . by mixing it with modern things" (20, 24). The complaint, however, seemingly directed at a mere undesirable compositional anachronism (things classical should not be mixed up with things modern), raises two distinct sets of questions.

The first derives from the compositional maxim presupposed by the 1886 "attempt": Why shouldn't—or in this case, at least, why should things classical not be mixed up with things modern? Any discussion of *The Birth of Tragedy* can very quickly acquire here misplaced quasi-theological overtones. One could say, for instance, that births and rebirths should be kept apart because explaining birth and explaining rebirth require altogether different kinds of arguments. Or, in a more sober mood, one can instead consider the fact that at least certain kinds of birth are derivative in their nature (i.e., are rebirths) is hardly compatible with the kind of organic analogy that powerfully unifies the first fifteen sections of *The Birth of Tragedy* (tragedy was born, developed, decayed, and died). The very notion of rebirth would be then deeply at odds with the emphasis Nietzsche puts on the sudden metempsychosis of Greek tragedy into Wagnerian opera. Nietzsche's 1886 "Selbstkritik" highlights in this respect, and against the latter part of the 1872 text, the supremacy of organic metaphors. In a famous passage, the notion of repetition (or at least of empirically produced repetition) is in fact demoted to the ranks of mere, laughable "metaphysical comfort" (22, 26).

The second set of questions, however, is of a different kind. The problem is, in fact, one of the coincidence between "self-criticism" and "rebirth," and indeed of the unintended analogy between self-criticism and rebirth, namely the fact that the refutation of the larger historical thesis on the rebirth of tragedy is achieved through the kind of new argumentative beginning Nietzsche himself calls "self-criticism." One could even say that, just like any "rebirth," every "self-criticism" reenacts the birth of argument, deliberately spoiling a grandiose former problem by mixing it with modern things. All of this allows us perhaps to tone down the pathos of the strict historical continuity of rebirth in the 1872 text by seeing that the introduction of rebirth in a historical explanation is in itself a strange anomaly, a critical anomaly that affects the explanation, as if every such explanation would, at that juncture, include a critique of its own contingency—a self-criticism. But then one could apply the same argument to self-criticism and connect such attempts with attempts at having one's argument born again, as it were. If this is so, then not only would self-criticism be a form of rebirth (even if rebirth is here rebirth by negation), but the metaphysical topic of rebirth itself would be bound to become self-critical at some point.

A convenient example of this complex structure is provided in the 1886 edition by the linear, unobstructed transition between the "Versuch einer Selbstkritik" and the enthusiastic 1872 "Vorwort an Richard Wagner" ("Preface to Richard Wagner"). Notwithstanding its being the emblem of the 1872 thesis on the rebirth of tragedy, the preface is kept in the 1886 edition as the first object of the "Attempt at Self-criticism," pointing thus to its own limits (by becoming the object of criticism) as well as to the limits of self-criticism itself (the "Attempt" having to include or quote the object of its critique). Another, perhaps less vivid, example is indeed the qualification Nietzsche applies to his own "self-criticism": a "Versuch," an attempt. Technically speaking, the 1886 "Attempt" is a "pre-preface," presented as the last chapter in a very intricate historical argument, in particular as the chapter through which the fiction of the possibility of starting da capo is enforced. But then again, and no less technically speaking, the 1872 preface is yet another, previous, last chapter, and so another, previous attempt at closing off another intricate historical argument.[3] One can then wonder whether the very question of rebirth is not always a question of an "attempt at." No less than "self-criticism," both "birth" and "rebirth" would emerge only as attempts, and problematic ones, at that.

The problem is not merely conceptual, as it becomes a serious problem in language that drives us back to our first set of questions. Indeed, Nietzsche was well aware in the 1886 "Attempt" that the ultimate consequence of mixing up old and new is a consequence in style, as his own apology for tragedy reborn—as well as, likely enough, tragedy reborn itself—is, in his own terms (and, one would like to add here, necessarily so), "badly written, ponderous, embarrassing, image-mad and image-confused [*bilderwüthig und bilderwirrig*], sentimental, in places saccharine to the point of effeminacy [*verzuckert bis zum Femininischen*], uneven in tempo, without the will to logical cleanliness, very convinced [*sehr überzeugt*], and therefore disdainful of proof, mistrustful even of the propriety of proof" (14, 19). This is a fairly accurate description of the 1872 book. It is also a fair description of the 1886 preface, which includes, among other ingredients, an apology for laughter, misquotes from Zarathustra, and quips at the "German people" ("a people who love drink and honor lack of clarity as a virtue," 20, 25). And, at least in part, it is also a description of itself, "image-mad and image-confused," if not outright "disdainful of proof." One could even be tempted to say that, by becoming critical, language is bound to become self-critical at some point. Language's becoming self-critical emerges precisely as an unfortunate attempt at being born again— that is, as an attempt against an alleged purity of style and so against an alleged purity of the discourse of self-reflection. The 1886 self-critical "Attempt" is therefore fully and unwittingly prefigured in the position of Wagnerian opera vis-à-vis Greek tragedy in the 1872 book. The continuity of historical development is thereby subjected to an important reversal, as the self-critical object can be said to prefigure its own critique.

Rebirth

The *Birth of Tragedy* that literary historians find enjoyable (that is, the first three-fifths of the book) appears to have everything to please literary historians: it reads like a disarmingly simple, unified explanation repeated in several parallel narratives. Whereas the latter repetitions tend to suggest an infinity of heuristic riches, the former structure is easy enough to grasp, and so not very hard both to teach and to refute. It has not been satisfactorily established, however, whether multiplication is tantamount to hidden complexity, just as it has not been established whether unified historical explanations are necessarily docile.

The best-known narrative belongs to literary history proper: after its birth "out of the spirit of music" (e.g., in the works of Aeschylus) Greek tragedy went through a period of decay (e.g., in those of Euripides) and died ("by suicide," 75, 76) at the hands of the so-called New Comedy, whose leftovers persist in the opera. The same process is paralleled in a simultaneous narrative of technical metamorphoses: the tragic chorus was brought onto the stage and acquired mimetic autonomy, a "discursive and discrete Apollonian action and characters," in Alexander Nehamas's words.[4] All alleged musicality was lost in the opera through procedures such as the recitative or the *stilo rappresentativo* in general. Simultaneously, in a third narrative, Nietzsche suggests that as soon as the chorus was brought onto the stage (whereas previously it had been off stage) the public was brought along with it, and audiences became able to detach themselves from, and so to measure, what takes place on stage: in a word, the critic was born, and tragedy became a matter of public opinion. Finally, in a fourth, and also very well-known, parallel narrative, the death and decomposition of tragedy and of the "Hellenic man" are said to be inversely proportional to the emergence of philosophy and the "theoretical man." Some of these narratives—especially the second and third—do not quite reach their conclusions until much later, as the full picture of a grim modern world shaped by opera, *stilo rappresentativo*, critical audiences, and philosophy will emerge only very near the end of the book. However, in the beginning of section 16 (the beginning of the notorious latter part of the book, apparently absent from earlier versions of the manuscript),[5] Nietzsche feels comfortable enough to provide a unifying meta-explanation that applies at least to his historical version of the development of tragedy.

"By this elaborate historical example," Nietzsche writes, "we have sought to make clear [*klarzumachen gesucht*] how tragedy goes to inevitable ruin with the disappearance of the spirit of music, how it could have been born only out of that spirit" (102, 99). Exactly what he has sought to make clear, Nietzsche adds some thirty pages later, is what was "bisher unerklärten," "previously unclear" (126, 119), namely the "change [*Umwandlung*] and degeneration of the Hellenic man" (ibid.) in what Nietzsche calls the "Socratic culture" (127, 119). The maximum degree of clarity coincides, in fact, with the lowest point in history, as what becomes fully illuminated is not so much a Hellenic past as modern "pessimism."[6] This is what the elaboration of every "historical example" ultimately amounts to. What is made clear can only be what escapes all clear perspective on

a narrative of history, and so Nietzsche's "historical example"—
namely what "is felt by [the Socratic culture] as the terribly unclear
[*das Schrecklich-Unerklärliche*] and the overwhelmingly hostile [*das
Übermachtig-Feindselige*]" (ibid.).

The economics of the historical example entails therefore an elu-
cidation of the present, seen in the strict temporal contiguity of the
argument as the future of an exemplary past. It depends accordingly
on an all-important previous guarantee according to which certain
past signs will be interpreted as clear and certain signs of a future.[7]
No wonder that Nietzsche's emphasis on the rebirth of tragedy is
first and foremost an emphasis on "the most certain auspices [*die
allersichersten Auspizien*]" (ibid.) drawn from his own description of
the final, "modern," stage of the development of tragedy, as well as
from the specific auspice-reading capability that tacitly goes with
the power of revision of the past. In fact, we find a correlation between three decisive terms: "the most certain auspices" cause to
"revive in us [*in uns aufleben*]" (ibid.) certain "hopes" as to the inevitability of a "rebirth." As with the *aues spectare* in the *auspicium*, all
inspection of the past depends on an analogy between what is inspected and what the inspected matter stands for. Hence, the *auf* of
aufleben and the *wieder* of *Wiedergeburt* contain the principle of
repetition that allows for the past to work as a sign, whatever this
may mean.

Except for "whatever this may mean" (to be illuminated at the
end of this section), the point is well known and hardly controver-
sial. More surprising, however, is the guarantee that allows the *auspex* to view his rebirth-watching activities with "hopes"—that is, to
frame the nature of the auspices under a metaprinciple of hope for
the grim "modern world" (ibid.), or, in short, to be sure that there is
something to look forward to. The fact is surprising, given the very

catastrophic nature of the historical example and the bleak overtones of the final stage of the historical explanation itself. Rebirth-
watching, then, implies a solution for the problem of the discontinuity between a catastrophic narrative that works as an example to
be read and the hopes for a not so catastrophic future. Such a solution presents itself as a particular form of reading, namely as a mix-
ture of overcoming and destroying a previous example. The inspector will have to literally turn his birds inside out. (The *auspex* will
perhaps resemble a *haruspex*.) In any case, the inspector becomes
less and less a quiet believer in some (no matter how fantastic) form
of inference, and more and more literally an in*ferre*r, for whom the
future has to be taken out of the past necessarily by force of a specific operation—that is, for whom reading the past and producing
the future are hardly distinguishable. No past is therefore exemplary
for the *auspex*, in that the past is what gets destroyed by the constitution of the future and indeed by the constitution of a past-
according-to-the-future.

This perhaps undesirably truculent description has at least helped
me to get to a more sobering matter, namely to what I take to be the
decisive textual and compositional problem in *The Birth of Tragedy*.
I turn to it briefly (even if deviously). My analysis will purport to
suggest, as a closing introductory remark on the book, the kinds of
procedures through which things like the careful and all-encompass-
ing historical explanation of its first part are self-critically destroyed
in the second, complete with an implicit attempt at a doctrine on
self-critical destruction.[8]

This complex process coincides at one point with a peculiar use of
the concept of analogy: specifically, to denote the terms of the exemplary relationship between the history of Greek tragedy and the
history of both German philosophy and German music. At the very

end of section 19, Nietzsche writes:

> To what, then, does the mystery of this oneness of German music and
> philosophy point, if not to a new form of existence, concerning whose
> character we can inform ourselves only by surmise from Hellenic analo-
> gies [*über deren Inhalt wir uns nur aus hellenischen Analogien ahnend
> unterrichten können*]? In fact, to us, who stand at the boundary between
> two different forms of existence, the Hellenic model [*Vorbild*] retains
> this immeasurable value, that all these transitions and struggles are im-
> printed upon it in a classically instructive form—except that we more
> or less [*gleichsam*] analogically relive [*analogisch durcherleben*] the
> chief epochs of the Hellenic nature [*Wesen*] in reverse order [*in um-
> gekehrter Ordnung*] and seem, for instance, to be passing backward
> [*rückwärts . . . zu schreiten*] from the Alexandrian age to the period of
> tragedy. Moreover, we feel as if the birth of [another] tragic age would
> mean for the German spirit merely a return to itself [*eine Rückkehr zu
> sich selbst*], a blessed self-rediscovery [*ein seliges Sichwiederfinden*]. . . .
> Now, at last, after its return home to the originary source of its being
> [*nach seiner Heimkehr zum Urquell seines Wesens*], [the German spirit]
> may venture to stride along boldly and freely before the eyes of all na-
> tions without being attached to the lead strings of a Romanic civiliza-
> tion. (128–29, 121)

The passage appears to turn around the ambiguous attributes of
the "Hellenic model." In the "classically instructive" terms of that
model, we, "who stand at the boundary between two different
forms of existence," are guaranteed to "analogisch durcherleben"
"the chief epochs of the Hellenic nature." In this sense, a future
"form of existence" (i.e., the epoch of "another tragic age") will be
determined, through analogy, by a past "form of existence" (i.e., the
"period of tragedy"). This, of course, is what classics are for: to teach
by analogy.

The problem, however, is the inconspicuous adverb *gleichsam*,
"more or less." In this passage, "gleichsam . . . analogisch durcherle-

ben" means not so much (say) "practically relive through analogy" (which, after all, is compatible with some uses of *gleichsam*) as, literally, "analogically relive . . . in reverse order." The verb *durcherleben*, then, would have to mean here "relive in reverse order." The "umgekehrte Ordnung" is the inverted order of Hellenic analogies as a constitutive ingredient of the Greek "Vorbild"; it points not so much to all the other misleading *Kehre* in the passage (the "Rückkehr," the "Heimkehr," and ultimately the "seliges Sichwiederfinden" that will eventually coincide with a neo-Hellenic "form of existence" and end our Socratic misery in the comfort of home) as to another (conspicuous, but still very elusive) metaphor for "Hellenic analogy" in the passage, namely the coinage, the imprinting, of a model.

Indeed the whole passage seems to me to be built around an ironic usage of expressions such as "klassisch-belehrende Form," "classically instructive form," as if Nietzsche were suggesting that he presents a perfect analogy, from which much can be learned, provided one takes it upside down. All instruction proceeds here through the "umgekehrte Ordnung" of analogy, and so no *durcherleben*, and likewise no *Sichwiederfinden*, is of any help—or, indeed, is even possible, except as a "gleichsam durcherleben" or a "gleichsam Sichwiederfinden." This is ultimately why even the German spirit is bound, as Nietzsche adds shortly afterwards, and very humblingly so, to yield to the "high honor and rare distinction" (129, 121) of having to learn from the Greeks, "these highest of all teachers" (ibid.). Hence the "immeasurable value" of our Greek model, the immeasurable value of the coin where signs are coined: since it can reproduce itself only in a reverse order, it can never quite repeat itself; and so its value, being literally "immeasurable," will become a model that cannot be followed, an impossible direct order, analogy, teaching instruction—in sum, an unclear example.

Furthermore, the other example in the passage is not presented in the indicative mood, which would turn the extraordinary hypothesis of a "passing backward from the Alexandrian age to the period of tragedy" into a statement of fact, whose truth or falsity would then be at stake. Only outraged literary historians and elated ultra-Nietzscheans take such formulas seriously. Instead, the example is made to depend on a previous perception—"we seem, for instance, to be passing backward from the Alexandrian age to the period of tragedy [*wir . . . jetzt aus dem alexandrinischen Zeitalter rückwärts zur Periode der Tragödie zu schreiten scheinen*]"—which in the terms of that very passage can never prove to be more than mere appearance or a matter of opinion.

As remarked above, the *wieder* of *Wiedergeburt* contains the principle of repetition that allows the past to work as a sign. The problem is, however, that such a principle of repetition finally means that this past is "immeasurable." Indeed, all repetition is bound to the order of inverted analogy and so must appear as an unintended dissociation from the repeated past, and produce the past in the closed, parodic form of a historical explanation. That is, in a word, the relationship between (say) *Geburt* and *Wiedergeburt*, the first and the second part of *The Birth of Tragedy*, and the 1872 text and the 1886 "Attempt": the second term in all three pairs denotes a failed attempt at a specific form of repetition; and yet these attempts succeed, in that they cannot help producing a manageable past, contained in this case within the limits of a historical explanation. It is to such an explanation (and hence to the first part of the book) that we should now turn.

Birth

In the first part of the book, the dedication to Richard Wagner is followed by section 1. That section begins with the detailed description of the primal scene of birth that has done so much for the reputation of the whole book: the very scene of the birth of Attic tragedy. This scene, however, is interspersed with several remarks of a different kind:

> We shall have gained much for the science of aesthetics, once we conclude, not merely by logical insight [*nicht nur zur logischen Einsicht*], but by the immediate certainty of intuition [*sondern zur unmittelbaren Sicherheit der Anschauung*], that the further development [*Fortentwickelung*] of art is bound up with the Apollonian and Dionysian doubleness [*Duplicität*]—just as, in a similar way, generation depends on the duality of the sexes, on continuous strife [*bei fortwährendem Kampfe*], and so on only periodically intervening reconciliations. Those terms we borrow from the Greeks, as they make perceptible to the Insightful One the profound secret doctrines of their view of art [*Kunstanschauung*]—not, to be sure, in concepts, but in the intensely clear forms of the world of their gods. To their two art deities, Apollo and Dionysus, is tied our knowledge that in the Greek world there existed a tremendous opposition [*ein ungeheurer Gegensatz*], in origin and ends, between the Apollonian art of sculpture and the nonrepresentative, Dionysian art of music: these two different drives [*Triebe*] walk side by side, for the most part openly at variance with one another, and they continually incite each other to new and more powerful births [*zu immer neuen kräftigeren Geburten*], which perpetuate a conflict of opposites, only apparently bridged by the common word "art," until eventually, by a metaphysical miracle of the Hellenic "will," they appear coupled together, and through this coupling ultimately generate an equally Dionysian and Apollonian work of art—Attic tragedy. (25–26, 33)

The model narrative of birth (we will assume for the moment that there indeed is one) is in fact entangled in a sustained discussion in which several degrees and possibilities of access to knowledge are contrasted and evaluated, and several crucial categories (the Apollonian and the Dionysian, among others) are introduced. Both contrast and evaluation are polarized around two different characters, which do not belong in the narrative of birth proper: the first is the omnipresent but nondescript "we," and the second is the conspicuous "the Insightful One," "der Einsichtige." The beginning of the passage consists in a recommendation ("Wir werden viel . . . gewonnen haben, wenn wir . . .") which urges the initial "we" to behave like the second character in the passage: that is, to behave like the Insightful One.

Two courses of action are then recurrently presented, and that presentation is what is "epistemological" about the passage. The first course of action is that of "making perceptible . . . in concepts," announced earlier on as "logical insight." The only example of the consequence of this course of action is given shortly afterwards in the allegedly inadequate use of a single term ("art") to *überbrücken*, to "bridge," a perpetual "conflict of opposites" between "two different drives" (25, 27). The logical insight, like the subsumption in concepts, is a specific way of dealing with difference. Since this course of action is explicitly rejected (not much would be gained by following it, as the "we" declares in the beginning), the model for the second course of action ("the Insightful One") can be accurately described as having no use for logical insight. Indeed "logical insight" is contrasted with "immediate certainty of intuition." The opposition at stake quotes explicitly a known locus of post-Kantian philosophy, namely a peculiar mode of relationship between *Begriff* and *Anschauung*, "concept" and "intuition," and so between Understanding and Sensibility. Moreover, "immediate certainty" recalls the "immediate knowledge" at the beginning of Hegel's *Phenomenology of*

Mind. To quote Nietzsche's later remark on *The Birth of Tragedy*, in *Ecce Homo*: "It stinks of Hegel."[9]

A second opposition, concerning modes of knowledge-transmission, is contained in the phrase "the profound secret doctrines of their view of art [*Kunstanschauung*]." These are precisely what can never be made perceptible in concepts. Of course, a *Kunstanschauung* is a view of art, and any view of art can be called just that. This particular *Kunstanschauung*, however, is irreducible to concepts, and, as was made clear before, this can only mean that its "profound secret doctrines" can be made perceptible by "the immediate certainty of intuition [*Anschauung*]" alone. It is, then, not so much a thematized and independent vision as the product of *Anschauung* proper. In a sense, the reference to *Kunstanschauung* implies here a notion of art-as-intuition. One has here, of course, the classic opposition between esoteric and exoteric knowledge—tied, however, not so much to different levels of access to truth (e.g., those not requiring any special procedure and those requiring special procedures such as allegoresis) as to different, and incompatible, powers or faculties, namely the Sensibility and the Understanding.

One important qualification should be made at this point, however. Despite any Kantian references in Nietzsche's opposition between intuition and concept, "intuition," rather than denoting the product of sense perceptions, seems to refer here to a mode of privileged access to the truth, and so to a full-fledged faculty, namely a faculty in which differences are also bridged in concepts. A question arises, therefore, as to the content of intuitions. Enter then the "intensely clear forms of the world of [Greek] gods." In these forms nothing is bridged, as their intense clarity is what is apprehended by "the immediate certainty of intuition." Intuition can accordingly be defined as the power to make perceptible to the senses, with a superior degree of certainty, "intensely clear forms." Here, however, one would require a second qualification, one that my very functional analogy between intuition and concept hopelessly ignores. In fact, whereas in this passage the description of the working of the concept is tantamount to the description of a (no matter how misplaced) active operation of the mind (i.e., the operation characterized by the metaphor of "bridging"), the contents of intuitions are not so much products of the mind (and in that sense intuition is not really a faculty) as, in themselves, forms of worlds—that is, forms of things. Accordingly, the "science of aesthetics" so conceived appears to be endowed with a degree of objectivity that would be incompatible with any epistemology to speak of, as it would be, in its intensity and clarity, wholly independent from any construction. "Intensely clear forms" is thus a metaphor for the object of a science which does not derive from a power of the mind. Aesthetics is here the most likely candidate for such an extraordinary position.

The birth narrative, meanwhile, is dependent upon three different but closely related figures: a metaphor for development, which identifies the "further development of art" with a process of "generation"; a metaphor for polarity, which identifies "duality" with "doubleness" and even "duplicity [*Duplicität*]"; and a metaphor for the "Apollonian and Dionysian," identified with "the sexes." Even if at least the first and the last of these metaphors appear to naturalize the process so described in the general picture of a theory of movement governed by biological (and, indeed, organic) imperatives, the second metaphor introduces a first disturbance in this unified version, as it implicitly attributes to "duality" the quasi-moral implications noticeable in its equivalent "duplicity." It is not so much that the world of vital instincts is irreducible to moral evaluation (and thus is essentially duplicitous)—the point has often been made in regard to Nietzsche—as that this conceptual anadiplosis, compared by Nietzsche to sexual duplication, affects the very theory of movement that is being described. Indeed, and contrary to the pre-established harmony of most phylogenetic narratives, where there is no room for any uncertainty as to the destination of movement, this process does not appear to be predetermined, in that it includes an ingredient of uncertainty allowed by an originary duplication. So the passage cannot help making terms like "further development [*Fortentwickelung*]," seen as an instance of "generation," echo in subsequent descriptions of a "fortwährender Kampf" ("continuous strife"), turning generation into a matter of fighting (and hence the product of a constitutive factor of uncertainty as to the results of successive combats).[10]

As to the sexual metaphors concerning generation, it is certainly possible (but ultimately irrelevant) to follow throughout the book the not always congruent specifications of the candidates to parenthood (as well as to derive some passing comfort from the fact that, even if in the 1872 title tragedy is born "out of the spirit of music," in a preliminary 1870 fragment "the mothers of tragedy are named will, illusion, and pain"). Be that as it may, Nietzsche's main concern has not to do with the substance of seldom more than momentary prosopopoeiae. Rather, it has to do with the description of a set of possible relationships, a complex configuration of possibilities. Hence the rewriting of the "Apollonian and Dionysian doubleness" not only as "the duality of the sexes," but also, and more specifically, as "two different drives [*Triebe*]." In fact, these descriptions tend not to be made in terms of what categorical poles are, but rather in terms of what they can do—in terms of their might. The birth narrative is accordingly the narrative of the development of *Triebschicksale*, of the ever duplicitous destinations of two different drives.

In a first moment, they "walk side by side [*gehen nebeneinander her*], for the most part openly at variance [*im Zwiespalt*] with one another." (Incidentally, *Zwiespalt* prolongs here both the *Kampf* and the *Duplicität*.) Doubleness, however, to this first configuration, is much more than a theme: it is indeed the structural possibility of two elements both "[walking] side by side" and being "at variance with one another." In a second moment, the two elements "continually incite each other to new and more powerful births [*sich gegenseitig zu immer neuen kräftigeren Geburten reizend*]." Again, this seemingly straightforward description of an intentional action (such as would be the production of more creatures) is somewhat affected by the participle that marks the position of the narrator toward the story (*reizend*: "inciting," "stimulating," "exciting," "alluring," "irritating," "charming"). In fact, the agonistic overtones of previous descriptions suggest, if not the implausibility of peaceful courtship altogether, at least the ambivalence of the very intention to produce "births." In a third moment, the latter, "births," are said to "perpetuate a conflict of opposites." They become, indeed, conflict-produced, and become so in a perpetual way. Once more, births are contradictory, as all production—far from being a synthesis (albeit temporary) of previous conflicts—becomes a figure of sorts, where two conflicting sentences in a state of war are contained *tant bien que mal*.

In a way, the preceding narrative (or the narrative segment that precedes the birth of tragedy proper) also works as an explanation for the above-mentioned remarks on the inadequacy of the word "art." I observed that such a word was an example of the consequences of a course of action dictated by "logical insight." Now, the emblem of the failure of logical insight (the use of a "common word" to denote all Greek *Geburten*) can be seen as a figure for the logical problem of the impossibility of justifying the bridging of contradictions. Such bridging is always "nur scheinbar," "only apparent."

The first three moments of the birth narrative emphasize the lack of coincidence between two different drives (the Apollonian and the Dionysian), and indeed reinforce each other as well as reinforce the suggestion that such a lack of coincidence is the natural destiny of those two drives. This is why the birth of Greek tragedy, understood as the fourth moment in the birth narrative, is particularly ambiguous. From a structural point of view it is a moment of *Paarung*, of "coupling" of drives. Coupling, however, is what has never happened before, since the previous stages of the narrative are all characterized as stages of dissociation. It is, then, as Nietzsche calls it, "ein metaphysischer Wunderakt," "a metaphysical miracle" proper. A miracle here would be not so much an event endowed with a special salvational, redeeming, content as the very narrative form of structural impossibility: that is, a story of coincidence. At the same time, the "metaphysical miracle" is a quasi-epistemological allegory, as it ultimately denotes that there are no natural states of development (and hence no possibility of a priori reading the inscription of its laws in a succession of historical events), and so that the notion of *Fortentwickelung* does not correspond to any historical or organic necessity inscribed in its constituents, as it is an a posteriori, quasi-empirical label attached to what is perceived (by "the immediate certainty of intuition" of the narrating "we") to be a series of configurations deployed in time. Thus, the miracle is the event, as it takes place in this narrative as the impossibility of a destiny for both drives involved. In the birth narrative, the birth of tragedy is therefore the particular function through which the very idea of functionality—and so of historical cause and natural destiny—is made the object of derision: that is, historicized, reduced to the temporal form of an aesthetic event.[11]

There is, moreover, a specific fable of the miracle: the Attic tragedy is "generated" "by a metaphysical miracle of the Hellenic 'will' [*durch einen metaphysischen Wunderakt des hellenischen "Willens"*]." Whereas the metaphor of generation, in the terms of the previous stages of the birth narrative (again prolonging all organic and sexual analogies), suggests that the birth of tragedy is somewhat akin to a physical miracle, from the point of view of the structural impossibility of any causally determined production of the *Paarung* of drives, such a miracle is indeed achieved through a meta-act.[12] "Will" is the term Nietzsche uses to denote the protagonist of the specific class of acts I call meta-acts: acts that are figured as disruptions or as emblems of the inherent disruption of the possibility of a causal chain of events. The complex relations at stake in the notion of "a metaphysical miracle" are more explicitly deployed in a fragment of a previous version of the book:

> The fact that nature has tied the origin [*Entstehung*] of tragedy to these two fundamental drives [*Grundtriebe*], the Apollonian and the Dionysian, should strike us just as much as an abyss of reason as the provision of that same nature to tie propagation [*Propagation*] to the doubleness [*Duplicität*] of the sexes, about which the great Kant never ceased to be amazed. The secret they have in common is that two mutually hostile principles can give rise to something new where these conflicting drives appear as one [*in dem jene zwiespältigen Triebe als Einheit erscheinen*]; in this sense propagation, in the same way as the tragic work of art, can be considered an assurance [*eine Bürgschaft*] as to the rebirth of Dionysus, like a radiance of hope on the eternally mournful face of Demeter.[13]

Kant's amazement, in the passage above, just like the *Wunder* of the final version of the text, is indeed an amazement directed at a meta-act, the common secret of the birth of tragedy and sexual reproduction. Even if the structural role of "will" is played here by nature, one should not disregard the fact that, no matter what term is used, the structural subject of meta-acts is constituted by the inscription of "two mutually hostile principles," just as the meta-act consists in a temporal *Paarung* of these hostile principles. Whether in the realm of the "artistic powers [*kunstleriche Mächte*]" (30, 38) or in the realm of the "artistic drives of nature [*Kunsttriebe der Natur*]" (31, 38), the meta-act of birth is the production of a coincidence (a "periodically intervening reconciliation [*Versöhnung*]")—which, however, by definition cannot be explained a priori, let alone predicted.

This discussion necessarily takes us to the unequal status of nature and will, and indeed to the very metaphoricity of organic metaphors in Nietzsche's description of the process of birth. In fact, even if the innumerable references to "generation" and "birth" be taken at face value, one must still account for the definitely nonorganic description of birth as the product of an act of will. Since that act of will is contrary to the putative will of the drives involved (and so to the will of nature), the concept of "birth," as the concept of a *contra naturam* act of will, corresponds to the concept of intentional production of an artistic form. Miraculous genetics is in fact no more than a compendious name for a poetics: the domain wherein production is technically achieved through an act of will, the domain where the only form of art is artistic. From the point of view of those ensnared by Nietzsche's insistence on organic metaphors, of those who wonder at physical wonders and marvel at natural marvels, instead, the act of the production of a birth is what has properly to remain metaphysical: a meta-act.

The ambiguities contained in and by the notion of "birth," just as those contained in the difficult notion of "producing generation," make it possible for us to detect, in Nietzsche's conception of the moment of birth, the moment both of the creation of specific products (the most "powerful" one being Attic tragedy) and of a specific problem.

The products are indeed the artistic forms that were *geboren* and which Nietzsche terms, metonymically, *Geburten*. He can, accordingly, declare that "the Dionysian and the Apollonian, in new births ever following one another and mutually enhancing each another [*in immer neuen auf einander folgenden Geburten, und sich gegenseitig steigernd*], controlled the Hellenic genius" (41, 47), evoking in "following one another" the very movement of *Fortentwickelung*, and in "enhancing each other" the process of *sich reizen*. As to the problem, to which I will now turn, it concerns the very substance of the product, the substance of artistic form. There are several available terms used to characterize different possibilities as to the substance of engendered products, such as "synthesis," "consequence," or even "compromise formation." And yet, as we shall soon see, none of them resembles even faintly Nietzsche's description of the problem. From the very first occurrence of the question in the book, in fact, the problem appears to be one of the "equally Dionysian and Apollonian work of art [*das ebenso dionysische als apollinische Kunstwerk*]," where indeed nothing is *aufgehoben* (since both drives are kept as such, and we only have a momentary coupling of conflicting forces) or a direct consequence of anything (except in a very general and trivial sense of the term). Nor is anything "reconciled" except momentarily; nor are there any lasting compromises to speak of.[14]

All that has been said precludes, in my view, a causal understanding of the function and, indeed, of the very notion of "art." On the one hand, and since artistic products are produced through "continuous strife," art cannot be said to a priori restore a putative lost balance; that is, it cannot be said to achieve such a restoration once and for all. (Restoration—if indeed one can speak of restoration—is at most the a posteriori description of a contingent moment in a fight.) On the other hand, the very perpetuity of the strife does not correspond to the instrumental function of a therapy. (Therapy—if indeed one can speak of therapy—is at most the description of an unintended effect of a *Fortentwickelung*, a temporal, continuous, further development.)

Nietzsche describes the complex relation between these two different drives as a "gegenseitige Nothwendigkeit," a "mutual necessity" (39, 45). The expression occurs at the conclusion of a short analysis of a well-known painting by Raphael, ambiguously titled *Transfiguration*. Nietzsche calls it a "gleichnissartiges Gemälde," a "parablelike painting." The ways of parable, however, are rather mysterious there:

> The lower half of the picture, with the possessed boy, the despairing bearers, the bewildered, terrified disciples, shows us the reflection of eternal originary pain, of the sole ground of the world [*die Wieder-spiegelung des ewigen Urschmerzes, des einzigen Grundes der Welt*]: "appearance" [*der "Schein"*] is here the reflection of eternal contradiction, of the father of things [*Widerschein des ewigen Widerspruchs, des Vaters der Dinge*]. From this appearance [*Schein*] rises upwards, like an ambrosial vapor, a visionlike new world of appearances [*eine visionsgleiche neue Scheinwelt*], which those entrapped in the first appearance do not see. . . . Here we have before our eyes, in the highest artistic symbolism [*in höchster Kunstsymbolik*], that Apolline world of beauty and its lower ground [*Untergrund*], the terrible wisdom of Silenus, and understand, by intuition [*und begreiffen, durch Intuition*], their mutual necessity [*ihre gegenseitige Nothwendigkeit*]. (39, 45)

If one forgets for a minute the context of doctrinal allusion denoted by Raphael's title,[15] transfiguration would be here the operation through which one world is converted into another, and so the operation through which the symbolic way of this particular painting is brought about. Nietzsche's description of the painting points, indeed, to the order of such a conversion in its distinct narrative structure. (From world$_1$ rises "upwards" world$_2$, just as in the painting itself two characters of world$_1$ point "upwards" to world$_2$.) "Mutual necessity" is in this sense little more than narrative necessity, as the latter narrative is the narrative of the construction of a symbolic link.

This causal version reemerges in the text in the final metaphor of the *Untergrund*, whereby "the reflection . . . of the sole ground of the world" becomes the under-ground of a "visionlike new world." One has here, however, a first ingredient which complicates the very causal structure of the narrative of transfiguration. In fact, not only is the relation between world$_1$ and world$_2$ one of symbolic causality as the very structure of world$_1$, allegedly also the ground of world$_2$ (and, in Raphael's painting, the literal ground of world$_2$), is itself produced through reflection: that is, it is symbolically produced. In other words, the ground not only has to be produced; it also has to appear. This latter feature accounts for the characterization of both worlds in terms of "appearance" and is incompatible with a simpler understanding of the painting in which world$_2$ would be understood as symbolized (indeed, reflected) by world$_1$, as it is equally incompatible with the concept of a grounding relationship between Apolline and Dionysian drives. As long as the ground has to appear, there cannot be any transfiguration, and so there cannot be any symbolic operation or equivalence. The "lower ground" is therefore not a ground but the mere appearance of a ground—indeed, the representation of what by definition cannot appear. (But then again, this means only that what we have—or, rather, have not—here is a painting.) From this point of view, then, mutual necessity is ontological identity, since the substance of all objects in Nietzsche's description of the painting is appearance. This is precisely what its being a painting (that is, an artifact) means: even "the terrible wisdom of Silenus" is always only apparent. The conclusion is, of course, that (*pace* Nietzsche, and in his own terms) there cannot be such a thing as a "gleichnissartiges Gemälde," or, better, that a parable-like painting is indeed a painting that is never quite like a parable.

Such is ultimately the reason why Nietzsche has to abandon his causal, symbolic understanding of the whole painting and provide metaphysical explanations as to the origin of its ground. From an epistemological standpoint this means abandoning the problematic notion of a form of conceptual knowledge without concepts (a "begreiffen, durch Intuition"), through which the contradictory possibility of understanding appearance is ideally preserved in the form of a narrative concerning the destiny of appearance (i.e., appearance moves upwards), and getting down to hard-core conceptual hypotheses. Analogous doubts can be cast on the epistemological function of allegoresis in his discussion of Raphael's *Transfiguration*: "The lower half of the picture . . . shows us the reflection of eternal originary pain, of the sole ground of the world [*die Wiederspiegelung des ewigen Urschmerzes, des einzigen Grundes der Welt*]." In fact, the allegorical meaning of the painting is what cannot be represented at all, namely "the sole ground of the world." It does not take a strict enthusiasm for the signifier to read under the concept of *Wiederspiegelung*, reflection, which accounts for the possibility of symbolic representation and which, simultaneously, points to the very possibility that is excluded by Nietzsche's arguments, a looming concept of countermirroring (of *Widerspiegelung*). In fact, the very text proceeds precisely in that direction, by explicitly substituting *wider* for *wieder*: "Der 'Schein' ist hier Widerschein des ewigen Widerspruchs, des Vaters der Dinge." To truly follow the turn of the text, one would have to literally retranslate (i.e., to allegorize) the passage: "The 'appearance' is here counterappearance of the eternal contradiction, of the father of things."

We are, then, driven back to the family romance of contradiction and inverted models, as well as to a somewhat undesirably vast meaning of "appearance." Will as the power to perform meta-acts is here "the father of things," as "counterappearance of the eternal contradiction" suggests the implausible coupling of two different drives. There is, however, a second form of contradiction, which does not admit of being reduced to the thematization of properties of ur-drives, let alone of archetypes. Such is the contradiction between contradiction itself and appearance: the fact that contradiction has to produce itself as appearance, and so that "the 'appearance' is here counterappearance." The beatific descriptions of the ambrosial vapors of "a visionlike new world of appearances" are, then, simultaneously not so beatific descriptions of the mixed ancestry of the vision, just as the tormented descriptions of "eternal originary pain" are bound to convert their object in yet another "visionlike new world of appearances." Pain and bliss alike, as Raphael knew well, are produced through painting—that is, they are merely picturesque. So the ground, as it emerges, will be converted in yet another theme. The symbolic substance of the ground, however, and paradoxically enough, is what triggers a potential regression that ultimately will never reach a ground.

The predicament so described is indeed not only the problem of the birth of tragedy but even that of birth in general, as both terms are used by Nietzsche in *The Birth of Tragedy*. Nietzsche himself was very well aware (namely in the "Attempt" of 1886, already discussed) that such was the kind of predicament bound to contami-

nate discourse itself, since in the end it is bound to affect all attempts at metaphor and example, especially when the notion of the
Dionysian is at stake. In fact, in the terms of Nietzsche's general
theory on the difference between the Apollonian and the Dionysian,
there cannot be any manifestation of the Dionysian (whatever it
may mean) except through purely Apollonian means—in a word,
through transfiguration. Only through symbol can the alleged force
of the Dionysian become sensible. Symbol alone can convey will.
The problem, of course, is that will in language is always represented
will, and so there will always be a moment of intentional construction of what I have been calling meta-acts, a moment when the highest possible meta-level is invented, and so calculable. There is, thus,
an important element of misprision in Nietzsche's interest for Attic
tragedy. What presents itself as an interest for a miraculous coupling
of originary drives is indistinguishable from an interest for an artistic
form said to represent that miracle, and thus for the very act that
denies any fundamental, grounding, import to that miracle.[16]

Necessary Supplements

In spite of all its likely maddening intricacies, my discussion in
the previous section has pointed to a rather simple (albeit technical)
conclusion, namely that, in Nietzsche's own terms, there can be no
concept of "representation of the unapparent," nor indeed any de-
piction of the under-ground of the aesthetic, that is not contradictory. What follows is that no amount of interpretation, complete
with the corresponding tropological paraphernalia, can do justice
(or, indeed, could ever do justice) to Nietzsche's ambitions in *The
Birth of Tragedy*. Moreover, the more adequate metaphors would
be, the more would grow the disproportion between Nietzsche's
metaphors and his intellectual intentions (even if "intention" de-

notes here a complex mix of philosophical, historiographical, literary, and philological ambitions).

This conclusion I use as a premise for the last, brief step of my discussion. In fact, the will (or what Nietzsche calls, in slightly more dignified terms, "the dark wisdom of Silenus") cannot emerge in metaphors; nor can it emerge—a phoenixlike vision often attributed to Walter Benjamin but actually fully Hegelian—from the ruins of metaphors; nor does it emerge from the production of ruins. Rather, I contend, in *The Birth of Tragedy* the will can only be what in a sense metaphors do not mean—that is, it can only coincide with the very awkward inscription of transfiguration in transfiguration.[17] As Nietzsche puts it ("a very important restriction" to his general thesis on the victory of the "highest intelligibility of drama" over music, 139, 129–30), "at the most essential point, this Apollonian illusion is broken and annihilated" (139, 130).

Since the core of Apollonian illusion would be here the possibility of a sense, a direction, in transfiguration (and so of a hierarchy of appearances), which ultimately would endow metaphors with a cognitive content, the breaking and, indeed, the annihilation of metaphor become a major interference in the general historical theory of the birth and rebirth of tragedy. Against such a theory (which, of course, is to a certain extent his own theory and, in the full extent, has to be Nietzsche's own theory for literary historians), Nietzsche offers the restricted possibility of "the difficult relation [*das schwierige Verhältniss*] of the Apollonian and the Dionysian in tragedy" (139–40, 130). Such a relation "may really be symbolized by a fraternal bond of the two deities: Dionysus speaks the language of Apollo; and Apollo, finally, the language of Dionysus; and so the highest goal of tragedy and of all art is attained" (140, 130). The passage, deceptively clear as it is, lends itself to some specific difficulties, as it suggests that the best possible symbol for a "difficult relation" is a "fraternal bond." The somewhat solemn final reference to the ultimate ends of tragedy and art is therefore made more sober by the particular nature of the bond, to the point that it can be read as almost straightforwardly ironical. The "highest goal" of tragedy is made possible by a difficult bond, indeed by an inextricable knot. Such a bond, in the terms of the metaphor in the passage, is linguistic: Apollo speaks the language of Dionysus, and Dionysus speaks the language of Apollo. Each god is defined in terms of his proper language; however, each of these languages requires a second god, who can be defined only in terms of the first. Both gods thus speak a foreign language. (Or, even better, the native language of each god is foreign in its very nature.) This structure is not so much one of the mutual linguistic understanding (nothing is said about the polyglot capacities of either Apollo or Dionysus) as it is one of the potential untranslatability of each god in terms of himself. Apollo is therefore translatable only in Dionysian, just as Dionysus has to be translated in Apollonian. The irony in the metaphor is, of course, that each god is only understandable in terms of the proper language of a second god—who, alas, has no proper language. The irony of the metaphor, meanwhile, runs even deeper: in fact, nothing is symbolized by it, as there is no way of establishing either an equivalence or a hierarchy between its terms—nothing is translated. Neither is "Apollo is Dionysus" false, nor is "Apollo [or Dionysus] is more powerful than Dionysus [or Apollo]" true. Thus are broken both the "Apollonian illusion" of a perfect transfiguration and the Apollonian illusion of a transfigurative operation for the concept of "perfect transfiguration."

The metaphor above complicates decisively some of Nietzsche's best-known insistences and metaphors that belong in the "theory" of the book, and that have been traditionally judged for their own specific meaning and cognitive content. It is incompatible, for instance, with the general theory according to which "the Apollonian element in tragedy has by means of its illusion gained a complete victory over the primordial Dionysian element of music" (139, 129), which is the most notorious literary-historical thesis in the book. It is also deeply at odds with a (somewhat different) general theory concerning the "genesis of the tragic myth" (151, 140), according to which both spectator and artist share "the complete pleasure in appearance and spectacle [*die volle Lust am Schein und am Schauen*]" and at the same time each one "negates this pleasure and finds a *still higher satisfaction* in the annihilation of the visible world of appearance" (ibid.). And last but not least, it complicates the very mode of Dionysian transcendence as well as the idea of an "artistic domain beyond the Apollonian" (to be achieved, incidentally, by transfiguration; Nietzsche uses the verb *verklären* [154, 143]), perhaps indeed the ultimate object of the "true artistic intention [*die wahre Kunstabsicht*] of Apollo" (155, 143). The Dionysian mode of transcendence is what provides the background for a teleological interpretation of the priority of the Dionysian, namely through the notion that the Apollonian is in the end a form of defense-mechanism become necessary "in order to keep the living world of individuation alive" (ibid.). An adjoining metaphor refers to the covering of Dionysian "dissonance" by a "veil of beauty [*Schönheitsschleier*]" (ibid.).

So one should be prepared not to go out on a limb with the encouraging proto-Zarathustrian thought of the "incarnation of dissonance [*Menschwerdung der Dissonanz*]" (ibid.) and the corresponding prophetic mood upon which the book concludes. (The passage in question occurs in section 25.) As a matter of fact, the former thought is itself fully contradictory, at least as long as the concepts of the Apollonian and the Dionysian are seen as corresponding to ontologically distinct objects, with distinct properties, distinct languages, and distinct domains. Indeed, the "Dionysian capacity of a people" (154, 143) is bound to become, ironically enough, necessarily dressed up to the point of anonymity by Apollonian veils: the veils of a large transfigurative theory which produce the kind of powerful interpretation that allows us to consider Nietzsche as the professional reincarnation of a Schleiermacher in his own right.

Ironically enough, the expression "incarnation of dissonance" can be retrospectively applied instead to the only character in the book who seems to lack any kind of Dionysian capacity. I am, of course, referring to Socrates. In the oversimplified historical fable against which I have been on and off directing my efforts, Socrates plays a very definite and unambiguous part. He is the "other spectator who did not comprehend tragedy and therefore did not esteem it" (81, 81), a third "deity" (83, 82), an "altogether newborn demon" (ibid.) who inaugurated a "new opposition" (ibid.: the Dionysian vs. the Socratic), which ultimately destroyed the art of Greek tragedy. Connected to that new opposition is what Nietzsche calls "aesthetic Socratism" (85, 83), whose general law is, still according to him, that "To be beautiful, everything must be reasonable [*alles muss verständig sein, um schön zu sein*]" (85, 83–84). Consequently, "wherever [Socratism] turns its probing eyes, it sees lack of insight and the power of illusion; and from this lack it infers that there is an intrinsic perverseness [*Verkehrtheit*] and objectionableness [*Verwerflichkeit*] to what exists" (89, 87). And, finally, the "demonic Socrates" (94, 91) is responsible for having exerted on Plato the kind of "pressure [*Druck*]" that has led the latter to proscribe poetry: "Here philosophic thought overgrows art and compels it to cling close to the trunk of dialectic. The Apollonian tendency has withdrawn into the cocoon of logical schematism" (ibid.).

At this point the fable closes. Not so Nietzsche. In a crucial passage toward the end of that same section (section 14) he alludes, somewhat elliptically, to a "profound experience in Socrates' own life" (96, 92) which "impels us [*zwingt uns*] to ask whether there is necessarily only an antipodal relation [*ein antipodisches Verhältnis*] between Socratism and art, and whether the birth of an 'artistic Socrates' [*die Geburt eines "künstlerichen Sokrates"*] is altogether a contradiction in terms." "Artistic Socrates" is provisionally defined as a contradiction, whereas the hypothetical structure of the passage indicates that such is probably the case; and, if so, it is also an inescapable contradiction as well as the emblem of the possibility of the rebirth of tragedy in the second part of the book. The construction of the corroboration of the hypothesis that will ensue obeys the precise program of section 25's prophetic—and failed—maneuvers: "If we could think dissonance incarnated . . ." (155, 143). That thought is both the topic of the corroboration and the actual expansion of the ellipsis contained in the phrase "profound experience":

> That despotic logician [i.e., Socrates] had occasionally in regard to art the feeling of a gap, a void, half a reproach, a possibly neglected duty [*das Gefühl einer Lücke, einer Leere, eines halben Vorwurfs, einer vielleicht versäumten Pflicht*]. There often came to him, as he told his friends in prison, one and the same dream vision [*Traumerscheinung*], which always said the same thing: "Socrates, practice music! [*Sokrates, treibe Musik!*]" Up to his very last days he comforts himself with the view that his philosophizing is the highest of the arts dedicated to the Muses [*die höchste Musenkunst*] and refuses to believe that a deity would remind him of the "common popular music." Finally, in prison, in order to thoroughly unburden his conscience [*um sein Gewissen gänzlich zu entlasten*], he does consent to practice this music, for which he

has but little respect. And in this mood he composes a hymn to Apollo and turns a few Aesopian fables into verse. It was something akin to the demonic warning voice that urged him to these exercises; it was his Apollonian insight that, like a barbaric king, he did not understand the noble image of a god and was in danger of sinning against a deity— through his lack of understanding [durch sein Nichtsverstehn]. The word of the Socratic dream vision is the only sign of any second thoughts [das einzige Zeichen einer Bedenklichkeit] about the limits of logical nature [über die Grenzen der logischen Natur]: Perhaps (as he must have asked himself) what to me is the incomprehensible is not necessarily the irrational [ist das mir Nichtverständliche doch nicht auch sofort das Unverständige]? Perhaps there is a realm of wisdom from which the logician is banned? Perhaps art is even a necessary correlative and supplement [ein nothwendiges Correlativum und Supplement] of science? (96, 92–93)

The narrative of Socrates' "profound experience" is the narrative of a particular "dream vision," followed by the attribution to Socrates of several consequences of such a vision, expressed in three questions that "he must have asked himself," according to the omniscient narrator in the passage. Such a vision is causally connected, in the narrative, with the initial reference to "the feeling of a gap, a void, half a reproach, a possibly neglected duty," as it is interpreted as a "sign" of "second thoughts" on what, in the terms of Socrates' standard role, is the fundamental opposition between art and science. It is a vision "about the limits of logical nature." The three final questions in the passage present, indeed, a reiterated rewriting of the model of that very opposition, a rewriting of the possibility of an "antipodal relation between Socratism and art." The first question dissociates the incomprehensible and the irrational, and so helps legitimize the notion of a domain for what is both incomprehensible and rational. Such a domain is easily identifiable as a topos of Romantic and post-Romantic thought; indeed, it is the kind of commonplace that is less congruous with the standard structural function of Nietzsche's Socrates than with Dilthey's later emphasis on two meta-realms and two distinct basic modes of knowledge. In the terms of this first question, therefore, "incomprehensible" does not necessarily mean "irrational," as the "limits of logical nature" are drawn by considering the possibility of a form of knowledge independent from "science." The name for the domain of that kind of knowledge is, of course, "art." The second question builds on the transcendental metaphor par excellence, the metaphor of a delimited field, by describing the limits of logical nature as the possibility of "a realm of wisdom from which the logician is banned." Only in the third question, however, is the trope of the "antipodal relation" explicitly rewritten, specifically in the obscure albeit conspicuous expression "necessary correlative and supplement." Since the poles of the relation so defined remain the same (art and science), as indeed the possibility of a relation between them remains untouched, the two decisive ingredients in the rewriting that takes place are "necessary" and "supplement." The first term, curiously enough imported from the realm of wisdom from which the logician is not banned, overdetermines the very relation by suggesting a sort of transcendental antipodism, and so not a mere empirical relation as a co-relation proper. The second term, also unexpectedly imported from the same realm, suggests a hierarchy between the poles, as art becomes a "supplement" of science. The particular flavor of the rewriting that takes place, then, derives from the specific association of two different moves which concentrate disparate terms inherited from a similar vocabulary (or from a similar standpoint) into a single complex expression: a movement of overstatement (*"necessary* supplement," I emphasize) and a movement of understatement ("necessary *supplement*," I emphasize again). It is not so much that, in the terms of Socrates' third question, there is no antipodal relation between art and science as that antipodism is both necessary and supplementary.[18]

This point brings us back to the dynamics of the "Traumerscheinung" in the passage, about which it could be said that this also is necessary and supplementary. The text is full of signs of the simultaneously contingent and necessary status of the picturesque apparition, to the point that it is marked by a disproportion between the description of Socrates' casual "second thoughts about the limits of logical nature" ("had occasionally in regard to art the feeling of a gap," "half a reproach, a possibly neglected duty") and the reiterated procedures of the vision ("one and the same dream vision, which always said the same thing: 'Socrates, practice music!'").[19] Accordingly, a strict economic explanation of the vision is not adequate (e.g., "The vision is the symptom of 'a gap, a void'"), just as, on the other hand, the vision is not a mere supplement to Socrates' standard predicates.[20]

Nietzsche's reference, then, to Socrates' "Apollonian insight" (the kind of insight that ultimately leads him to follow the instructions of the dream vision—that is, to follow a vision)[21] is a reference to a specific power that can achieve a particular form of articulation of necessity and supplementarity, whereby the lack of necessity in the "feeling of a gap" is supplemented by the acknowledgment of a necessary, imperious and imperative, nature to the vision's advice. There is accordingly a specific irony in this aesthetics of practical reason, so to speak, and one is not sure whether Socrates is immune to it. In the first place, the advice of the vision is understood and followed by Socrates *cum grano salis*, "in order to thoroughly unburden his conscience [*um sein Gewissen gänzlich zu entlasten*]": hence his consenting "to practice this music for which he has but little respect." In addition to that, one has to consider nevertheless the thoroughly ironical result of Socrates' following of the vision's prescriptions. The "noble image of a god" whom he does not understand, presumably Dionysus—at least if one connects the passage to the reference, in the immediately preceding paragraph, to "an antiDionysian tendency . . . which has received in [Socrates] an unheard-of and magnificent expression" (95, 92)—becomes at least in part a composed "hymn" to another God (Apollo), a hymn to practical considerations, and so yet another misunderstanding. Be that as it may, and if one is to follow here the famous prescriptions of the Platonic Socrates of the *Republic*, neither hymns (607a) nor (perhaps) fables (378e, 397d, 398b) are exactly threatening or, indeed, exactly musical. In a very general sense, of course, they are musical, just as, for Nietzsche's (and Plato's) Socrates, "his philosophizing is the highest of the arts dedicated to the Muses [*die höchste Musenkunst*]." The nongeneral sense, however, would coincide rather with what the same Socrates calls "common popular music," and with the musical modes Plato's Socrates associates with drunkenness, sloth, and idleness in general (*Rep.* 398d–399c). Be that as it may, Socrates' musical exercises, Platonic or Nietzschean, are in any case not Dionysian.

This kind of irony, which definitely emerges from a particular interference of necessity and supplementarity, prevents the description of Socrates' "profound experience" from being unequivocally read as the story of a decisive change of perspective (and so from working as an unambiguous exemplum). Accordingly, the complex metaphors of an "artistic Socrates," a "music-practicing Socrates" as an "incarnation of dissonance," are far from representing the revenge of music over philosophy (since that story is not what is actually told in the text), just as they cannot be compared to what, in the metaphor of bilingualism in section 21 (discussed above), would be an impossible conversion of languages. Rather, they point to a failed convergence, as they are bound to defer the possibility of their final meaning (and so of any kind of mutual, "harmonic" correlation) onto the untold future of a told story.

"Here," Nietzsche writes in section 15, "we knock, deeply moved, at the gates of the present and future: Will this 'reversal' ["*Umschlagen*"] lead to ever new configurations of genius, and especially of the music-practicing Socrates?" (102, 98). The answer provided by the second part of *The Birth of Tragedy* is yes, since the "gates of the present and future" have been laboriously constructed in the first part of the book as the products of a past, invented through historical explanations, complete with decisive moments of birth, death, and reversal. This affirmative answer, however, entails the consideration of its own supplementarity. So it is definitely not surprising that the final promise of the 1886 "Attempt" ("You ought to learn how to laugh, my young friends. . . . Then perhaps as laughers you may someday dispatch all metaphysic comforts to the devil—metaphysics in front," 22, 26), by concluding a past achieved through a critical exegesis of *The Birth of Tragedy*, requires yet another future.

It has become current for us to see exegesis and interpretation as movements through which supplements are produced. It has even become acceptable to acknowledge that such supplements are necessary. Less so, however, that by producing what they supplement, they become the second part, the supplement, of what they produce. If I am right, therefore, Nietzsche's philological dreams of pasts resurrected, presents corrected, and futures improved, which affect both his concept of *The Birth of Tragedy* and the alleged "theories" in the book, end up by engendering mere attempts at correction that can be read in the history of the book—without, for that matter, acquiring any decisive prominence. They are indeed the metaphysician's worst nightmare.

FOUR

The Roots of Invention

Times appear to favor invention, or, at least, books with the word "invention" in the title (a somewhat recent epidemic).[1] As invention as a concept triumphs, one seems to witness the ebb of concepts such as mimesis or imitation. With very few (remarkable) exceptions,[2] realism (i.e., the doctrine according to which some things at least are found, not made) is hardly a popular topic for philosophers, writers, and critics. Whereas in 1978 Nelson Goodman admitted that, by using titles such as "The Fabrication of Facts,"[3] he was "irritating those fundamentalists who know very well that facts are found, not made,"[4] no one would have imagined that two decades later assertions of this kind would, at the very most, stir mild indignation in some quarters. So probably the need (or the temptation) has come to irritate some more recent fundamentalists about the fact that, in an important sense, some things can never be made. Such, however, will not be my task in this final chapter. I will be dealing with a few problems concerning the notion of "something made" instead, specifically through the metaphor of invention.

The term "invention" seems to have acquired two major, though not necessarily incompatible, uses. On the one hand, there has arisen a demystifying, pessimistic use, as when one says, "See? It was never always there; it was invented." The status of invention, however, and as a rule, falls short of this notion of invention. Apparently, invention seems to have been always there all along—that is, it seems not to have been invented. The same could be said about "demystification" and "critique," which present us with the strange instance of optional imperatives that in most quarters seem to be treated as part of the very nature of things. On the other hand, of course, "invention" has a constructive, optimistic use, closer to a tribute to tireless human ingenuity, as in, "The Swedes invented a cure for depression," closer to a specific (and, again, noninvented) faculty of coping with problems: it is, so to speak, a trait of the essential dignity (or at least a trick of the trade) of humankind.

Apart from these uses, "invention" also performs a recognizable function these days, namely the ultimate function of subsuming facts and events alike under cultural categories. At a more abstract level, this is the function—to use Goodman's phrase without Goodman's irony—of trying to conceptualize the very fabrication of facts (and of describing the darker regions of the socially repressed in the process). In this sense, it is the invented nature of both facts and events that turns them into an instance of the omnipresence of the cultural. All forms of culturalism, one could say, are characteristically constructivist: that is, they tend to rely on uses such as those of "invention" described above.

It is amazing that such an extreme form of idealization of language, institutions, and societies (not to mention the mysterious term "agency") is first and foremost the trademark of contemporary traditions of cultural materialism, as if the desperate need to protect the status of a critical subject were achieved at the cost of demoting everything else to the dubious category of things made or fabricated. In the end, "made" means only more recent than a given, central position of the subject, indeed more recent that the critical consciousness of the subject. It could very well be that all pious tributes to the motley gods of cultural criticism will remain entrapped in an undesirable notion of expression as long as the position of the analyst as an utterer of truths everybody else can live by (especially if these are critical truths) does not itself come under closer scrutiny. The problem, however, is that such scrutiny would cause the loss of the considerable political power that cultural criticism mistakenly professes to have achieved, as well as the loss of the ultimate excuse for cultural studies, namely that they are not "merely theory." In fact, assuming that one can follow political injunctions at all, no one would follow the political injunctions of a disempowered subject. Here one might pause and simply suggest that the term "invention" be dropped, altogether. After all, it may very well be that the term, according to Wittgenstein's remark, "has to be withdrawn from language and sent for cleaning—then it can be put back in circulation."[5] But, of course, this will not do, as no word will vanish by sheer force of the power of mind.

Even if "invention" is often paired with words such as "culture," its most popular pairing is undoubtedly with "interpretation." Indeed, "invention" has come to be understood as a quasi-obligatory conceptual correlate of "interpretation," in that "interpretation" has come to denote the process through which what will count as the facts is actually fabricated. (Interpretation is generally considered to be the process through which the matter of the facts is established, so to speak.) The ebb of mimesis (to which I was alluding above) means in this respect that, at least for the time being, the realist days of interpretation, the days in which interpretation could be seen as the reproduction of a past meaning, seem to be over. But, despite all shrill laments to the contrary, only apparently did the attack on realism come in the shape of relativism or radical historicism. Indeed, culturalism can aptly be defined as a "new realism" of the subject, one in which the very literality of interpretation is removed from scrutiny and interpretation is seen as, in Stanley Fish's approving expression, "the only game in town." Now, what would be interesting would be to show what happens when you think of interpretation as the only game in town, as indeed when you think that there is only one game in town. It would have been enough, one might argue, to read Plato's *Republic* to imagine what such a town would be like.

I shall be taking, however, a different path. In fact, I propose to follow closely the implications for the notion of invention of Immanuel Kant's *Critique of Pure Reason*, namely those related to Kant's doctrine of a critical mode. These two concerns I take to be connected with the notion of interpretation, or rather with a specific version of the relation between criticism and interpretation in which criticism (in Kant's sense a remote but not altogether false cognate of "criticism" in expressions such as "literary criticism") is described as the refusal to grant either any sort of naturalness or any sort of contingency to interpretation. Kant's suggestion is twofold: (1) that what we now call interpretation has to be produced through *heuresis*—that is, invented—and (2) that invention proper is a topic whereby a traditional partition of faculties becomes completely impracticable, and necessarily so. As we will see, the incompatibility between Kant's two suggestions becomes especially noticeable in Kant's hesitations concerning the role and the status of the faculties (namely, but not exclusively, the Reason and the Imagination). Kant's text is admittedly a peculiar choice. In fact, the first *Critique* does not belong in the canon of hermeneutics (let alone in that of literary or cultural studies), either as a central text or as an esteemed, albeit misled, precursor. Perhaps this incongruity will grant me the modicum of outrage or curiosity that will prevent the readers from abandoning their reading while trying to make it through the rather technical analysis that will follow.

Production and Imitation

If, as Jacques Derrida once wrote, "an invention always presupposes some illegality, the breaking of an implicit contract[, and] inserts a disorder into the peaceful ordering of things, . . . disregards the proprieties,"[6] then one of the most current forms of such illegality is temporal inversion, in particular the suggestion that what most people believe was there before something else—usually some rough notion of "things as they really are"—was, indeed, there only after that something else. At the very end of the *Critique of Pure Reason*, in the chapter "The Architectonics of Pure Reason," Kant contrasts the figure of the philosopher with someone "who has actually learned a system of philosophy."[7] The latter, he writes,

> knows and judges only according to what was given to him. Contest him a definition and he does not know where to find another. He has educated himself after a foreign reason [*Er bildete sich nach fremder Vernunft*]; however, the faculty of imitation is not that of invention [*das nachbildende Vermögen ist nicht das erzeugende*]—that is, his knowledge does not derive from Reason, and even though it is undoubtedly, objectively, rational knowledge, it is, subjectively, merely historical. He has grasped it and has retained it well enough: that is, he has learned, and is a plaster cast of a living man [*ein Gipsabdruck von einem lebenden Menschen*]. (B864)

The passage appears to connect learning with what Kant calls "merely historical" knowledge. Anticipating some of Nietzsche's later attacks on this form of knowledge, the final metaphor (as well as the final irony, achieved by omitting all causal connection between learning in general and becoming a plaster cast ["Er hat . . . gelernet, und ist ein Gipsabdruck"]) connects historical knowledge (and its emblem, a death mask of life) to a specific faculty: the faculty of imitation, "das nachbildende Vermögen." Imitation (*Nachbildung*) is a fairly current term in the first *Critique* and is in this sense always historical. Moreover, it is temporally determined: if the term were to be translated literally, one would have to account for the prefix (*nach-*, "after-") in the German original. One imitates after something or someone. The order of historical knowledge can thus be said to be the specific temporal order of imitation. An additional pun, absent from my translation, increases the irony mentioned above. My sober and anodynous "he has educated himself after a foreign reason" sacrifices the etymological and morphological allusion in the German text: "Er *bildete* sich *nach* fremder Vernunft" (my emphasis). In so doing, it has to dispense with Kant's mischievous paraphrase of the verb *lernen*, "to learn" as "building oneself after [someone]." Indeed, to learn, by being learning after someone, is always to copy someone. The temporal order of learning is therefore the temporal order of imitation, and the irony of imitation is indeed the irony of all learning: doing something for the second time—the famous *Bildung*, "education," is "subjectively," as Kant says, always *Nachbildung*, and, as such, it reasserts the foreignness of what is imitated, of the model. In brief, for Kant (as for Plato), imitation is always inadequate, and that is why it is so curiously funny and unreasonable (producing plaster casts of something or someone that is still around, aping something or someone).

To the faculty of imitation Kant opposes "das erzeugende Vermögen." I have translated the phrase as "the faculty of invention." "Invention," however, is a deliberate concession to my topic: it is not altogether adequate (though by no means unacceptable in this context). Be that as it may, I am not interested so much in an opposition between imitation and invention as in the two different temporal orders presupposed by the two powers here involved: the power of plaster-casting life, so to speak, and the power of producing life itself. The temporality of the second power reads like the inversion of the temporality of the first, in that one does not produce *nach* anything, even if one produces "aus Vernunft," "from Reason." What does it mean, then, to be a philosopher (as opposed to learning philosophy historically)? As Kant adds shortly afterwards, in a characteristic tone, for Reason-like reasons you cannot really be one (at most, you can "learn to philosophize," B865). In fact, the philosopher is an *Urbild*, an original or an originary model, and, unfortunately, you can become only either what already was (through imitation after some model) or, as Nietzsche would put it, what you are (through self-invention). Philosophy is thus a specific kind of *Erzeugung*, of production, in whose temporality the origin of imitation is produced in advance, so the philosopher is always ahead of the after-builders—that is, is foreign to them. Unlike the mathematician, the physicist, and the logician, the philosopher is not, as Kant says, an "artist of Reason" but "the lawgiver of human Reason" (B867). To philosophize, then, is to produce the moment before the law—indeed, to give the law of Reason. Interestingly enough, not many professional philosophers have espoused a maximalist version of Kant's thesis, which one would associate instead with well-known Romantic descriptions of the figure of the poet, the *poietes*, who indeed does not imitate but is the "unacknowledged legislator of the world," in Shelley's famous phrase. As it happens, the phrase, after all, might have been given to him by Kant.

The criticism of the notion according to which learning consists in imitating someone is closely paralleled in the same chapter by the criticism of the notion according to which reading a scientific text consists in imitating its author's "description." There is an empirical reason for that: "One finds that the author [*Urheber*] and often even his late successors [*Nachfolger*] are wrong about an idea [*um eine Idee herumirren*], which they have not managed to make clear to themselves, and that hence they cannot define [*nicht bestimmen können*] the proper content, the articulation (the systematic unity), and the limits of science" (B862). There are, however, nonempirical reasons also:

> All sciences, being conceived [*ausgedacht*] from [*aus*] the standpoint of a certain general interest, have to be explained and defined not after the description given by their author [*nicht nach der Beschreibung, die der Urheber derselben davon gibt*] but after the idea [*nach der Idee*] which one finds in [*aus*] the natural unity of the parts, which he has brought together, and which is itself founded in Reason [*in der Vernunft*]. (Ibid.)

One would like to pursue the analogy between ur-things and remark that, just like any *Urbild*, the author (the *Urheber*) cannot be imitated. The point, however, is that the author is not the author or, rather, that the author can, but should not, be imitated. What Kant calls the *Urheber* here is merely what (somewhat paradoxically) "brings together . . . the natural unity of the parts." This bringing together is, however, derivative, in that it has to depend on the copresence of what is to be brought together. Accordingly, the author's descriptions are not to be trusted; that is, the author's gift is not to be taken. What is "natural" to science is precisely that copresence, what Kant calls elsewhere the "articulation," the "natural unity of the parts." Such a unity is founded in Reason. In it, one can find the idea. There is therefore the priority of a unity grounded in Reason against the version of such a priority as provided in authors' descriptions. The opposition is again well known as one between formalist and intentionalist accounts of interpretation, in particular between accounts in which intrinsic properties explain interpretation and accounts in which interpretation produces intrinsic properties. Needless to say, Kant seems to side here with formalism.

The problem, however, is that, just as the author is not the author, so what one would nowadays call the unity of form is not as natural a unity as Kant appears to be suggesting. Indeed, Kant's emphasis on what one would call, after both the New Criticism and analytic philosophy, the intrinsic analysis of an argument, a text, or a system is indissociable from an emphasis on the specific, privileged origin of what was defined as a "natural unity," namely Reason. Even if the "natural unity of the parts" of science is founded in Reason, science itself does not necessarily derive immediately from Reason. Science derives from an idea, and the possibility of such an idea is due to Reason. But science is conceived ("ausgedacht") "from [aus] the standpoint of a certain general interest." The *Ausdenken* of science is due to this unspecified prior interest. The interest is inscribed by Reason in an idea to the point that by proceeding after such an idea, interpretation is on a par with authorship, as it is a parallel *Zusammenbringen* of the text.[8] Interpretation, then, just like authorship, is more like a particular instance of a general interest, and the matter here is that there can be no imitation of the general by the particular. To such (failed) imitation one usually gives the name metonymy. But all metonymy is bound to appear as a specific, construed configuration of a local equivalent for a general, absent, and irreplaceable content.

Kant's curious theory is that only repeated, and presumably failed, descriptions can yield an adequate image of the idea of a science. In other words, only a series of partial *Nachbildungen* of an idea can produce an adequate equivalent of that idea. Since no guarantee exists as to the logic of such a series, only the temporality of repetition can explain production:

> It is regrettable that only after having spent a long time following the orientation [*nach Anweisung*] of an idea deeply hidden in us, collecting in a rhapsodic way, as building materials, many kinds of knowledge related to it, and even long after having technically put together [*technisch zusammengesetzt*] such knowledge, can we at last see the idea in a clear light and sketch a whole architectonically after the ends of Reason [*und ein Ganzes nach den Zwecken der Vernunft architektonisch zu entwerfen*]. (B862–63)

The opposition between collecting and sketching is reiterated at several other levels, namely as an opposition between proceeding "in a rhapsodic way" or "technically" and proceeding "architectonically." It is not merely an opposition between passive and active (since the technical *Zusammensetzung* is hardly a passive activity). Rather, it is the complex relation, causal rather than oppositional, between proceeding "nach Anweisung" (by following and orientation) and producing something "nach den Zwecken der Vernunft" (after the ends of Reason). No following of instructions (empirical, i.e. rhapsodic, or technical) as such will ever allow one to *entwerfen*, "sketch," anything. Only the repeated following of instructions will produce an adequately clear picture. In other words, the whole has to be produced, even if production is temporally determined by partial reproductions of a previous *Anweisung*. "Systems," adds Kant in a no less curious simile, "appear to be built like worms, through a *generatio aequivoca*, from the mere confluence of collected concepts [*Zusammenfluß von aufgesammelten Begriffen*], mutilated at first [*anfangs verstümmelt*], and, with time, complete" (B863).

The structure of the problem occurs in seemingly unrelated

(thematically or otherwise) passages of the text. Earlier on, in the "Transcendental Dialectic," in a passage kept only in the first edition, the opposition between imitation and invention permeates the distinction between several uses of language or, rather, between several kinds of objection (dogmatic, critical, and skeptical), which correspond to different possible attitudes toward language in a philosophical debate:

> Both the dogmatic and the skeptical objections must attribute to themselves in advance an insight on their object [*müssen beide so viel Einsicht ihres Gegenstandes vorgeben*], enough to assert anything about it, affirmative or negative. Only the critical objection is of such a nature that, by merely showing that one has invoked in support of one's assertion something that amounts to nothing or is merely imaginary [*nichtig und bloß eingebildet*], it thereby overthrows the theory [*die Theorie stürzt*], as it takes away from it its so-called foundation, without otherwise being willing to decide anything about the nature of the object [*Beschaffenheit des Gegenstandes*]. (A389)

The first two kinds of objection are characterized as having to incur some sort of petitio principii in order to work: they have, in a sense, to occur after something has been given. (And their specific illegitimacy for Kant, of course, lies in the fact that what has already been given was given by them.) Hence, dogmatic and skeptical objections can both be described as imitations. The third kind of objection, which Kant calls "critical," consists in an immanent analysis of both dogmatic and skeptical arguments, rather than in the thematizing of an alternative (thus reproducing a "theory" by having to decide something about the nature of an object). This third kind of objection, therefore, destroys the very opposition between alternatives that constitutes the ground of a "theory." In doing so, the critical objection points to the ideal of a groundless analysis, thereby, through immanent analysis, producing the very possibility of immanence *stricto sensu.* In this sense, critical analysis appears to be a critique of transcendence, and so a critique of imitation. I now turn, then, to a close analysis of Kant's arguments on the possibility of such a critique, which he elsewhere (viz. B451) calls "skeptical method."

Critical Skepticism

The basic opposition between "immanent" and "transcendent" is sketched in a notorious passage (where, among other things, "transcendent" is distinguished from "transcendental"), at the beginning of the "Transcendental Dialectic." The term "transcendental dialectic" is particularly misleading, especially if one follows the all-too-obvious analogy with "transcendental analytic," the first part of the "Transcendental Logic." Indeed, Kant's transcendental dialectic is defined from the outset as a set of critical objections directed against the very idea of a transcendental dialectic. Since dialectic is described as a "logic of the apparent [*Logik des Scheins*]" (B349),[9] the object of a transcendental dialectic is the concept of "transcendental appearance [*transzendentaler Schein*]" (B352). "Human Reason," Kant writes in his "Appendix to the Transcendental Dialectic,"

> has a natural tendency [*einen natürlichen Hang*] to transpose [*zu über-schreiten*] that frontier [the frontier of possible experience] so that transcendental ideas are so natural to itself as categories are to the Understanding, only with a difference: whereas the latter lead to the truth [*zur Wahrheit*] . . . the former can produce only an irresistible appearance [*unwiderstehlichen Schein bewirken*], whose illusion can hardly be stopped by the sharpest critique. (B670)

Transcendence is thus defined as a particular form of transposition, a *metapherein* achieved by "actual principles that purport to tear down all barriers and to attain a whole new territory that knows no demarcation anywhere" (B352). Such a transposition is the source of two typical kinds of error, as Kant calls them, which indeed correspond to two different forms of transposition, and so to two forms of imitation. The first (the error of the *ignava ratio*) consists in conferring a constitutive role to the idea of a supreme being and deriving therefrom the supremacy of an "authoritative verdict of a transcendent Reason" (B718). Accordingly, the Reason is lazily left without a proper task, as all that takes place is ipso facto a confirmation of a presupposed mandatory verdict. The second error is the error of the *perversa ratio* or the *hysteron proteron rationis*: "One turns things around and begins by taking as a ground the reality of a principle of purposive unity . . . and by anthropomorphically determining the concept of a higher intelligence . . . and then one imposes ends upon nature, in a violent and dictatorial way" (B720).[10] Both errors turn around the idea of an exemplary—and apparent, according to Kant—thematic and mimetic relationship between Reason and nature, as well as paralleling the distinction and the affinity between dogmatism and skepticism: in the former case, nature is determined as a recurrent illustration of a transcendent presupposition; in the latter, "the concept of a higher intelligence" is anthropomorphically reduced to the status of yet another transcendent presupposition—"the reality of a principle of purposive unity," indeed a mimetic and metaphoric principle.

The relation between error and truth, however, as well as the relation between transcendence and immanence, is considerably complicated by Kant's own arguments, to the point that, here again, one would hesitate to call it a mere opposition. All analysis of the notion of immanence would have to point out, from the outset, that, and despite all emphasis on its "mistaken" character, transcendence derives from a "natural tendency" of Reason and so, at the most, Reason has inscribed in itself both a transcendent and an immanent tendency: a mimetic faculty, comparable to Aristotle's (e.g., *Poet.* 1448b), and a mimeto-critical faculty, comparable to Plato's (e.g., *Rep.* 607b–c)—a power to produce illusions and a power to describe illusions as produced. Such powers are in fact inextricably tied together in Reason, since, according to Kant, "a priori we have to attribute to things necessarily all properties that constitute the conditions under which alone we can think them" (B405). Thus, even the reference to objects of possible experience that establishes the criterion of immanence proper depends on "certain anthropomorphisms" (B725) which are in this sense necessary, stemming in particular from the necessity "to regard the arrangement of the world as if it were springing from the intention of a Supreme Reason [*aus der Absicht einer allerhöchsten Vernunft*]" (B714). Such is a condition for what Kant calls the "reading" of experience proper, as opposed to mere "spelling": "Plato remarked very clearly that our faculty of cognition feels a higher need than that of spelling [*buchstabieren*] mere phenomena according to a synthetic unity in order to be able to read them as experience [*um sie als Erfahrung lesen zu können*]" (B370–71).

The passage above alludes to a specific hierarchy of faculties, as it suggests that the Understanding is incapable of reading experience by itself or, rather, of reading something as experience. On the one hand, reading presupposes a reference to the end of reading, which can be achieved by Reason alone. Such reference is to an intention. On the other hand, since what is read is always read as something, intention is therefore a figure for the end of reading, whose metaphoric nature is explicitly and repeatedly underlined. In fact, the forgetfulness of the metaphoric nature of the end of reading is a trait common to, and the specific link between, dogmatism and skepticism. Critical reading depends, therefore, on the acknowledgment of both the necessary and the metaphoric character of all transposition, as it depends on a specific function of Reason. The principle of such a function Kant calls the "law of specification [*Gesetz der Spezifikation*]" (B685). This law, independent from experience, is presupposed as a meta-principle of difference. "As a matter of fact," Kant writes, "we can have understanding only under the presupposition [*Voraussetzung*] that there are differences in nature, as well as under the condition [*Bedingung*] that nature's objects have a similarity [*Gleichartigkeit*] between themselves" (ibid.). By producing both the former presupposition and the latter condition, the Reason

> prepares the field for the Understanding (1) through a principle of similarity of the diverse [*ein Prinzip der Gleichartigkeit des Mannigfaltigen*] under higher genera; (2) through a fundamental law of the variety of the similar [*einen Grundsatz der Varietät des Gleichartigen*] under lower species; and, to complete the systematic unity, it adds, moreover, (3) a law of affinity of all concepts [*ein Gesetz der Affinität aller Begriffe*], which requires a continuous transition [*einen kontinuierlichen Übergang*] between species, through a gradual increase of diversity. We can call them the principles [*Prinzipen*] of the homogeneity, the specification, and the continuity of the forms. The latter results from the union of the two former, inasmuch as one has completed in the idea the systematic connection [*den systematischen Zusammenhang*], both in the ascent to higher genera and in the descent to lower species; for all diversities are related to each other [*unter einander verwandt*] as they descend from a single higher genus through all gradations of an ever extending determination. (B685–86)

In Kant's terminology (itself burdened with metaphors drawn from several sciences, particularly from chemistry), the three principles above, as well as the "law of specification" as a whole, are examples of an immanent use of transcendental ideas, in that such a use, even if it cannot be grounded in experience, real or possible, is a use presumably directed at experience, at the "field" of the Understanding. Moreover, those appear to be principles from which several (if not all) distinct features of scientific cognition can be derived, namely comparison, generalization, classification, description, and even inference. They are also, however, as such, figures of transcendence, specifically of the kind that renders possible the constitution of what is defined as "immanent." The homogeneity of forms corresponds to the synecdochic rule of genus: that is, to a given description of the participation of particulars in a class, through which is warranted a priori the overcoming of difference, through the appurtenance of every form to a level whereby formal difference is made irrelevant, as the specific articulation of genus and species is produced. The specification of forms corresponds to a principle of illustration through which it is also a priori warranted that, just as every part has its whole, so no whole is partless. Both homogeneity and specification, in Kant's text, produce a specific circulation of terms through which it is asserted that just as the diverse is similar (the so-called "Gleichartigkeit des Mannigfaltigen"), so the similar is varied (the so-called "Varietät des Gleichartigen"). As for the third principle, that of the continuity of forms—it stands for the general possibility of "a single higher genus." The continuity at stake there is not simply what exists in common between the two first principles— namely the very circulation between general and particular, part and whole, concrete and universal—but what could never be the object of experience, namely an a priori affinity of forms. In fact, Kant adds shortly afterwards, "one can easily see that this continuity of forms is a mere idea . . . not only because species are actually divided in nature . . . but also because we cannot make any determined empirical use of this law, since it does not show us the least sign of affinity [*Merkmal der Affinität*]" (B689).[11] What distinguishes these posi-

tions from the positions of both dogmatics and skeptics is that dogmatics and skeptics alike "believe that their judgment comes from
an insight of the object, when it is simply grounded in a greater or
lesser devotion to . . . principles [*auf der größeren und kleineren An-
hänglichkeit an . . . Grundsätzen*]" (B695)—that is, they blindly
yield to the natural *Hang*, "tendency," of Reason toward transcendence.

Kant notes accordingly that

> What is remarkable about these principles [*Prinzipien*: i.e., the three
> principles of the law of specification] . . . is that they appear to be tran-
> scendental, and, although they contain just simple ideas for the ob-
> servance of the empirical use of Reason, which use can follow only as if
> asymptotically [*nur gleichsam asymptotisch . . . folgen kann*]—that is,
> only approximatively, without ever attaining them—they possess never-
> theless, as synthetic a priori propositions, an objective, albeit undeter-
> mined, validity, and serve as a rule for the possible experience, being in
> fact used felicitously as heuristic principles [*als heuristische Grund-
> sätze*] in the very elaboration [of experience], even if no transcendental
> deduction can be brought about, since the latter . . . is always impossi-
> ble in relation to ideas. (B691–92)

These principles are what Kant also calls "heuristic fictions [*heurist-
ische Fiktionen*]" (B799), connected to "the hypothetical use of Reason [*der hypothetische Vernuftsgebrauch*]" (B675). From this standpoint, both the dogmatic and the skeptic, examples of the transcen-
dence-oriented *Hang* of Reason, partake no less of the inclination to
treat fictions as if they were true. Kant's diagnosis, however, does
not have to presuppose a privileged access to the truth, as in the end
all truth depends on the *heuresis* of fictions—that is, on the invention of fictions that is the specific task of Reason. Critical philosophy
depends instead on a privileged access to a theory of fiction, which
can be provided only by a transcendental philosophy understood as a

particular form of description of the confusion between truth and fiction. Such is the function of Kant's "Transcendental Dialectic," whose main and decisive procedure is that of organizing the distinction between "transcendence" and "immanence." That distinction can be justified only in the terms of a special kind of awareness, or the awareness of a special kind of description, which is critical proper.

As such, the critical philosophy of a transcendental dialectic, as a philosophy of hypothesis, will invariably come to resemble its main target, appearance, since the construction of hypotheses is the construction of the apparently true—the only kind of truth available. No wonder, then, that it intermittently maintains an awkward relation with both dogmatism and skepticism (and thus with *ignavitas* and hysteron proteron), since all hypothesis has to balance a thetic component against the understatement of the status of all thesis, the thesis against the hypo-, just as the use of Reason is, in Kant's mathematical metaphor, asymptotic. The figure of the "asymptotisch folgen" is precisely the figure of such a balance: always thetic, but never reaching a thesis. This means only that, for Kant's critical philosophy, immanence has to be invented, produced as a heuristic fiction—that is, produced transcendently and so as an object for critical philosophy. Here too, criticism awkwardly has to produce its own phenomenal text, or at least the fiction of intrinsic properties.[12]

Monograms

It is perhaps possible to recognize in the rigorous Kantian description of the relationship between transcendence and hypothesis some of the main methodological problems (both as a set of themes and as a proleptic description of their shortcomings) of what was later to become the hermeneutic tradition after Schleiermacher. On the one hand, Kant's description marks the entrance, as an explicit topic, of the necessary presupposition of an idea (an ersatz term, "prejudice," eventually became a compliment under Gadamer's Heideggerian theory of hermeneutics), "of the form of a totality of knowledge, which precedes [*vorhergeht*] the determined knowledge of the parts, and which contains the conditions to ascribe a priori to each part its place and its relation with the remaining parts" (B673)—in short, the notorious hermeneutic circle. On the other hand, however (and here is why the said tradition regresses from Kant), Kant refuses to grant such a principle any apodictic status, in which "the general is already certain and given in itself" (B674). Rather, the general remains, for Kant, always problematic, "a mere idea" (ibid.), or, as we would perhaps say, a fiction: "The particular [*das Besondere*] is certain, but the generality of the rule concerning this consequence is still a problem" (ibid.). In this sense, hypothesis is always subdued apodeixis, a weak proof that has inscribed in its terms and procedures its fictional origin. Fiction could therefore be functionally defined as a construed skepsis of inference, whereby meaning, history, and language lose all naturalness and are treated like products: to use rigorously Kant's rigorous vocabulary (which would only reemerge in the 1870's in the early essays of a certain young German philologist), fiction is the form of language as well as the possibility of history.

The crucial matter here, then, is the matter of the construction of a problematic relationship between what is given and what has to be presupposed. This amounts to the problem of the structure and of the order of *heuresis*, in particular, in Kant's own words, of the construction of "an essential a priori plurality and arrangement of parts [*Mannigfaltigkeit und Ordnung der Teile*], determined by the principle of the end [of the idea]" (B861). Indeed, in this kind of determination one has a particularly intricate relationship between production and imitation, as, even if problematic (i.e., heuristic), the relationship between part and whole would remain up to a certain point bound by analogy. Such is the main difference between the "ideals of Reason" and the "creatures of Imagination":

> [The ideal of Reason] must always be based on determined concepts and serve as a rule and as a model [*Urbild*] either for observance [*Befolgung*] or for evaluation [*Beurteilung*]. Altogether different is the case of those creatures of the Imagination [*Ganz anders verhält es sich mit denen Geschöpfen der Einbildungskraft*], which no one can explain or provide an intelligible concept of, similar to monograms, which are made up from only a single line, that no alleged rule can determine, and that are more like a suspended sketch [*schwebende Zeichnung*] in the middle of diverse experiences—as those that painters and physiognomists claim to have in their heads, and that have to be a noncommunicable silhouette of their productions or evaluations—than like a determined picture [*ein bestimmtes Bild*]. (B598)

In fact, the comparison between "the ideal of Reason" and "a determined picture" is made in the terms of their ground, as they both must be "based on determined concepts." The determination of the concept is, so to speak, the ground of analogy (as well as the ground of this analogy). Determined pictures, curiously enough, in the passage above, are not produced by painters, especially not in their heads. Painters and physiognomists (here synecdoches for the *Einbildungskraft*, the Imagination), rather, produce "productions," "creatures," or "silhouettes," "which no one can explain or provide an intelligible concept of"—that is, "monograms." Since it cannot be imitated, a monogram, therefore, is not a model, an *Urbild*, as there are no rules concerning either its "observance" or its "evaluation." An *Urbild*, as Kant will argue in the following section, is a *Prototypon*: that is, something made for determined imitation. A monogram, instead, is more like what Kant calls in the third *Critique* a *Hypotypon*:

that is, something whose imitation is undetermined and therefore unintelligible—a "noncommunicable silhouette," or, in Kant's own only half-intelligible simile, a suspended (or floating) sketch.

The opposition between "picture," "model," and "prototype," on the one hand, and "monogram," on the other, appears thus to draw a distinction between Reason and Imagination (which is perhaps the distinction between the heads of philosophers and the heads of painters, as well as between imitation and production, public and private lawgiving). When, however, much later, in the next-to-last chapter, "The Architectonics of Pure Reason," Kant is again confronted with the question of the problematic (as opposed to apodictic) analogy between part and whole, brought about by hypothesis and so by heuristic fictions at large (specifically by architectonic fictions), he tends to recur to vocabularies and descriptions which he had previously proscribed.

The most notorious case is perhaps that of the term "scheme [*Schema*]," which had already been used profusely in the famous first chapter of the "Analytic of the Principles," entitled precisely "On the Schematism of the Pure Concepts of the Understanding," which deals with the role of the Imagination. The scheme is there "a third term," which "must be homogeneous [*in Gleichartigkeit stehen muß*] with the category, on the one hand, and, on the other, with the phenomenon, and . . . thus makes possible the application of the former to the latter" (B177). In itself, "it is merely a product of the Imagination" (B179). But whereas the "image [*Bild*]" is "a product of the empirical faculty of the productive Imagination" (B181)— meaning that images are invariably empirical illustrations produced by the Imagination (Kant's famous example is ". . . . ." as an image of the number five)—the scheme is "a product and as if a monogram of the pure a priori Imagination, through which and after which [*wodurch und wornach*] images become first possible" (ibid.). Without such monograms, Kant adds, images "are never fully congruous [*nicht völlig kongruieren*]" (ibid.) with concepts. Schematism corresponds, therefore, to the very possibility of a pure congruence, as Kant would put it, and is defined (again in a very famous passage) as "an art hidden in the depths of human soul, whose true mode of operation we will hardly ever be able to take away from nature and have unconcealed before our eyes" (B180–81).

As it happens, however, and as Kant develops his own theory of fiction into a theory of the ends of the productive structures of *heuresis* (i.e., an architectonics), he tends increasingly to see Reason under the figure of Imagination. Only this otherwise unexpected metaphorics would explain Kant's concept of an architectonics of pure Reason:

> What we call science can appear [only] architectonically, from affinity and through derivation from a single supreme and inner end, which first makes the whole possible [*der das Ganze allererst möglich macht*], and whose schema must contain, according to the idea—that is, a priori— the outline [*Umriß*] (*monogramma*) and the division [*Einteilung*] of the whole in parts [*Glieder*]. (B861–62)

Indeed, the above passage deals primarily with what in the chapter "On the Ideal in General" (analyzed above) would be a contradiction in terms, namely with a schematism of Reason, or, as the metaphor again recurs, a monogrammatism of Reason. This time, Reason appears to side with painters and physiognomists, in that it appears to owe its specific power (the power to construct science architectonically) not to "a determined picture" (B598) but, rather, to "those creatures of the Imagination, which no one can explain or provide an intelligible concept of" (ibid.). Such a monogrammatic power, *pace* Kant, reunites the heads of philosophers with the heads of sketchers, perhaps laying the ground for the specific (and para-doxical) affinity of the treatise and the sketchbook as philosophical genres.[13]

To describe a little further this monogrammatic power, one has to look closer at the very functioning of this schematism of Reason. The scheme as a figure achieves simultaneously two things. On the one hand, one has to have a transcendent synthesis of some sort, or, even better, a transcendent hypo-synthesis, a transcendent subdued syn-thesis, as it were. In its terms, the figure of the whole is hypo-thetical, and is given in the chapter "The Architectonics of Pure Rea-son" by the metaphor of the *Umriß*, the "outline" or *monogramma*. This latter term corresponds, meanwhile, to a metaphor for the very possibility of hypothesis. It contains both the thesis (when it is un-derstood as a particular emblem, as *gramme*) and its subduing (when it is understood as an approximative, imperfect, one-line sketch, as *mono-grammos*). On the other hand, the schema provides for a tran-scendental analysis, as it proleptically points to the very possibility of a dismemberment of the whole (what Kant calls, in a different con-text, at the beginning of the "Transcendental Analytic," a *Zerglied-erung*, a "decomposition" or "dismemberment" proper: B89)—that is, to "the division [*Einteilung*] of the whole in parts [*Glieder*]" (B861–62).

In an important respect, then, we are forced to read the first *Cri-tique* backwards, as the description of Reason in the "Transcenden-tal Dialectic," through metaphors such as that of the monogram, leads us in a way to the description of the Imagination in the "Tran-scendental Analytic" and possibly to a consideration of the hetero-geneity of Imagination and Understanding.

Subdued Syntheses

The most extensive section of the *Critique of Pure Reason*, indeed the largest part of the work by far, is the "Transcendental Doctrine of the Elements" (B31–B732). Therein Kant considers two main parts (*Teile*), corresponding to "two branches of human knowledge, possibly originating from a common root, albeit unknown to us, namely Sensibility and Understanding" (B29). The first part, relatively short (B33–B73), is the "Transcendental Aesthetic," as it is called, and deals with the Sensibility proper—that is, the way "objects are given to us" (ibid.). The second part, entitled "Transcendental Logic," concerning how "objects are thought" (ibid.), includes in turn two divisions (*Abteilungen*)—the "Transcendental Analytic" and the "Transcendental Dialectic," corresponding roughly to two different faculties, the Understanding and the Reason.

The question of the difference between Understanding and Reason is crucial ("The concepts of the Reason [*Vernuftbegriffe*] serve the purpose of conceiving [*dienen zum Begreifen*], just as the concepts of the Understanding [*Verstandesbegriffe*] serve the purpose of understanding [*zum Verstehen*] [perceptions]," B367) and a notorious *morceau de bravoure* of Kantian commentary. Whereas the latter concepts are "reflective [*reflektierte*]" ([B366] in the sense that the Understanding can be defined as the faculty of understanding perceptions), the former concepts are "conclusive [*geschlossene*]" ([ibid.] in the sense that Reason can be defined as the faculty of conceiving "something to which [*worauf*] the Reason leads in its conclusions [*in ihren Schlüssen*] from experience, and from which [*wornach*] it assesses and measures [*schätzet und abmisset*] the degree of its empirical use, without, however, amounting to its being a member of the empirical synthesis" [B367–68]). Presumably to emphasize the difference between Understanding and Reason, Kant will shortly afterwards (B368) substitute the term "transcendental idea" for the term "concept of the pure Reason." Just as "category" was the term used in the "Transcendental Analytic" for the pure concepts of the Understanding ("reine Verstandesbegriffe"), so "idea" is the term used in the "Transcendental Dialectic" for the concepts of pure Reason ("Begriffe der reinen Vernunft"). (The difference, in fact, rather than being merely between Understanding and Reason, seems to be double: on the one hand, between Understanding and *pure* Reason; on the other, between *pure* concepts and concepts.)

Be that as it may, and however crucial differences are—and they *are* crucial—the fact is that the two divisions of the "Transcendental Logic" tend to be described in analogy with one another. Not only is there what one might call a very obvious structural analogy between the two divisions (the pair "concepts" [i.e., "ideas"]/ "dialectical reasonings" in the Dialectic corresponding to the pair "concepts"/ "principles" in the Analytic, the homology between the three species of the "inferences of the Reason [*Vernuftschlüsse*]—categorical, hypothetical, and disjunctive—and those of judgment in general as described in the Analytic, and so forth), but the characterization of each division (and of each faculty) is often made in terms of metaphors that also occur in the other division, to the point that, except for their phenomenal occurrence in the text (which in itself is hardly proof of anything), one would hesitate to attribute to either of the divisions the primacy in the literal use of such metaphors. In the terms of the Introduction (already quoted), that is probably what it means for both Understanding and (pure) Reason to be a single "branch," indeed one of the two "branches of human knowledge." And, just as Kant speculates about the "common . . . albeit unknown" root of the Sensibility and the Understanding, my point of departure in this section will be that of a common root between Understanding and (pure) Reason, in the trivial enough sense (a purely literary sense, if one prefers) that at least some descriptions that apply to the latter are also used with respect to the former.

A conspicuous metaphor in Kant's description of the Understanding, in the first edition of the work, is the metaphor of lawgiving. This metaphor, as we have seen, is also prominently used in the "Transcendental Dialectic" apropos the philosopher, "the lawgiver of human Reason [*der Gesetzgeber der menschlichen Vernunft*]" (B867). Much earlier on, however, in the Analytic, Kant writes:

> The Understanding is not merely a faculty of rulemaking through comparison of phenomena [*ist . . . nicht bloß ein Vermögen, durch Vergleichung der Erscheinungen sich Reglen zu machen*]: it is itself lawgiving for nature [*die Gesetzgebung vor die Natur*]; that is, without the Understanding there would be no nature at all—that is, no synthetic unity of the diversity of phenomena according to rules. (A126–27)

Again, the opposition is one between analogy—comparison or even mimesis proper (*Vergleichung*)—and production, specifically the engendering of law. In fact, the phenomena cannot yield any mimetic *Anweisung*, any orientation; no rule can be derived, therefore, from a "comparison of phenomena." (In a strict sense, phenomena cannot be compared, as "they cannot be found outside ourselves, since they exist only in our Sensibility" [A127].) The knowledge of nature is achieved, to paraphrase a familiar expression from the Dialectic, after the ends of Understanding: "All phenomena as possible experiences lie a priori in the Understanding," in particular, in what Kant calls the unity of apperception.

The description of the functional structure of the unity of apperception (which is itself, in the famous Kantian definition, "the objective unity of all [empirical] consciousness in a consciousness"

[A123]), moreover, is achieved as the description of the production of "necessary consequences" of the former unity. These consequences can be subsumed under a general principle, which again takes us back (or forth) to the "Transcendental Dialectic":

> There must, then, be an objective a priori principle [*ein objektiver . . . a priori . . . Grund*] . . . whereon rest the possibility and indeed the necessity of a law [*Gesetz*] extensive to all phenomena, which consists in envisaging them thoroughly as sense data [*sie nämlich durchgängig als solche Data der Sinne anzusehen*], associable in themselves [*an sich assoziabel*] and subject to general rules concerning a transitional connection [*durchgängige Verknüpfung*] in reproduction. Such objective principle of all association of phenomena I call the affinity [*Affinität*] of these same phenomena. (A122)

Again the description is that of the giving of a law, namely the law through which phenomena become sense data. Such a description implies a second (and perhaps more conspicuous) description, of the very principle of the givenness of sense data: indeed, the principle of the law. Kant calls it the principle of the affinity of phenomena. The situation is once more that of a structural homology between the preparing of the field for the Sensibility by the Understanding (achieved through a prescribed affinity of phenomena: i.e., "All that is given to you is a priori 'associatable'") and the preparing of the field for the Understanding by the Reason, discussed in the "Transcendental Dialectic," through the so-called law of specification and, specifically, through "a law of *affinity* of all concepts [*ein Gesetz der* Affinität *aller Begriffe*]" ([B685] i.e., "All that is thought by you is a priori 'associatable'" through what Kant calls "a continuous transition [*ein kontinuierlicher Übergang*]" [ibid.]). In both cases (the "transitional connection [*durchgängige Verknüpfung*]" in the Analytic and the "continuous transition [*kontinuierlicher Über-*

gang]" in the Dialectic), it is a question of a "run" (*Gang*), a sequence whereby difference is a priori ruled out by a law of affinity. And even if, in the Dialectic, such a law is very explicitly considered to be a presupposition (as opposed to its objective nature as far as the Understanding is concerned), doubts remain both as to the presuppositional character of the law of the affinity of concepts and as to the objective character of the law of the affinity of phenomena. In fact, affinity as a metaphor, predicated differently in either case, introduces a disturbance concerning the literal sense of the term "affinity." Such a disturbance allows us to retain a presuppositional element in what is otherwise said to be a necessary consequence of the unity of apperception (thus allowing us to see the latter unity as produced) as well as to retain an objective element in what is said to be a cause of all inferring, through the Reason (thus allowing us to integrate the production of heuristic fictions in the context of an objective spontaneity). In either case, an uncertainty remains as to what each use of the term was supposed to clear out, namely the ground (i.e., the principle) of affinity.

The only really explicit doctrine concerning affinity in the first *Critique* is to be found in a passage of the first edition which immediately follows the passages discussed above, and in the terms of which "the affinity (close or distant) of all phenomena is a necessary consequence of a synthesis in the Imagination [*Synthesis in der Einbildungskraft*], which is grounded itself a priori in rules" (A123). According to this doctrine, the "objective principle of all association of phenomena" (A122) is produced by the Imagination through a specific operation Kant calls "synthesis." Indeed,

> The Imagination is therefore also a faculty of an a priori synthesis, wherefore we give it the name "productive Imagination" [*produktive Einbildungskraft*], and insofar as, with respect to all diversity of phe-

nomena, it has no other purpose but the necessary unity [of phenomena] in the synthesis, it can be called the transcendental function of the Imagination. Strange as it may seem, it becomes clear from the previous [conclusion] that only by means of this transcendental function of the Imagination can the affinity of phenomena [*Affinität der Erscheinungen*] and, with it, the association [*Assoziation*] and finally, through the latter, the reproduction after laws [*Reproduktion nach Gesetzen*], and therefore the experience itself [*die Erfahrung selbst*], become possible: since without [the transcendental function of the Imagination] no concepts of objects in an experience would quite flow together [*gar keine Begriffe von Gegenständen in eine Erfahrung zusammenfließen würden*]. (A123)

The function of synthesis can therefore, according to Kant's curious choice of words, be defined as the transcendental production of a *Zusammenfließen*, of a flowing together of concepts and given objects, which allows "two extreme ends [*beide äußerste Enden*], namely Sensibility and Understanding, to necessarily articulate [*notwendig zusammenhängen*] with each other" (A124). Indeed, this flowing together or "association" of concept and object presupposes a necessary articulation of faculties whereby "reproduction after laws" and so experience become possible. Synthesis is thus the production of no less than the transcendental articulation of mimesis that makes knowledge possible. As the Imagination is in this respect the faculty of synthesis, the ultimate consequence is simply that all possible knowledge is necessarily produced by the Imagination as "an active faculty [*ein tätiges Vermögen*] of the synthesis of a diversity" (A120), as the *Hang* of the Imagination, again like that of the Reason, is to make things transcendently *zusammenhängen*. The Imagination is therefore, as Kant puts it, "a fundamental faculty of the human soul that is the a priori ground of all knowledge [*ein Grundvermögen der menschlichen Seele, das aller Erkentnis a priori zum Grunde liegt]*" (A124). "That the Imagination is a necessary ingredient [*ein notwendiges Ingrediens*] of perception: here is something that no psychologist has ever thought" (A120n), soberly remarks Kant, right as usual, in a footnote. That "the Imagination [is] a blind albeit indispensable function of the soul [*eine blinde, obgleich unentbehrliche Funktion der Seele*]" (B103): here is something later poets have also maintained.

The topic of the Imagination as an "active faculty" is possibly the most conspicuous, even if by no means the easiest, topic in Kant's treatment of the Imagination in the second edition of the first *Critique*. Most of it occupies section 24 of the "Transcendental Deduction of the Pure Concepts of the Understanding," entitled "On the Application of Categories to Objects of the Senses in General." Kant's arguments presuppose a preliminary distinction (made explicit only a few pages into the section) between two kinds of Imagination and so between two kinds of synthesis. Given that, in general, "the Imagination is the faculty of bringing forth [*vorzustellen*] an object, even without its presence in the intuition" (B151), the distinction is made along the lines of the very difference between imitation and production. One has, then, on the one hand, the synthesis of what Kant calls "reproductive Imagination": this kind of Imagination "is merely subject to empirical laws, those of association, and therefore does not contribute to the explanation of the possibility of the a priori knowledge, pertaining therefore not to transcendental philosophy but to psychology" (B152). Just as *Nachbildung* is a pedagogical, subjective matter, so reproduction is here a matter of empirical syntheses fit for psychology. On the other hand, one has the kind of synthesis which belongs to "productive Imagination [*produktive Einbildungskraft*]" proper, which Kant calls "transcendental synthesis of the Imagination" ([ibid.] as opposed to "the mere intellectual connection [*Verbindung*]" of the *synthesis intellectualis*, which does not involve the Sensibility). Kant defines the transcendental synthesis of the Imagination as "an effect of the Understanding upon the Sensibility [*eine Wirkung des Verstandes auf die Sinnlichkeit*]" (ibid.). The notion of "effect," which occurs elsewhere in the "Transcendental Analytic,"[14] appears to be connected to the notion of production, in that it denotes a consequence of production, namely its product. What is "affected [*affiziert*]" (B154) by such a synthesis is what Kant calls the "inner sense" (ibid.), that is, the "form of intuition" (ibid.)—and hence the reason why this kind of synthesis is "an effect . . . upon the Sensibility":

> [The] determined intuition . . . is possible only through the conscience of the determination [of its inner sense] by the transcendental act of the Imagination (synthetic influence of the Understanding on the inner sense [*synthetischer Einfluß des Verstandes auf den inneren Sinn*]). (Ibid.)

The transcendental synthesis of the Imagination consists, therefore, in the determination of phenomenal sense, which is achieved through the production of the form of sense as such. In this specific and crucial respect, the "synthetic influence of the Understanding on the inner sense" is a meaning-attribution process through which the Understanding (or *Verstand*) actually serves "the purpose of understanding [*zum Verstehen*] [perceptions]" (B367)—that is, simultaneously produces the form of perception and determines the interpretation of perceptions. This *Verstehen*, then, cannot be more or less than both the production through the Imagination of the form of a phenomenally manifested object and the attribution of a meaning to such a phenomenally manifested product of the Imagination. In this sense too, interpretation can be characterized as a process of "synthetic influence" through an act of the Imagination. "This act,"

Kant adds, "I have called 'figurative synthesis' [*figürliche Synthesis*]" (B154).

This conspicuous expression occurs for the first time a few pages earlier:

> This synthesis of the diverse of sensible intuition, which is a priori possible and necessary, can be named "figurative" (*synthesis speciosa*), to be distinguished from the kind of synthesis that, with respect to the diverse of an intuition in general, would be thought in the mere category, and that is called "connection in the Understanding" [*Verstandesverbindung*] (*synthesis intellectualis*); both are *transcendental*, not only because they proceed a priori but also because they ground a priori the possibility of other knowledge. (B151)

The synthetic influence is thus figurative. In Kant's text, *figürliche* translates *speciosa*, which means both "ornate" (in the sense that the *stilus ornatus* is a traditional correlate of the *stilus figuratus*) and "unreal" (in the sense that *species* is opposed to *res*). The term *species* usually translates *eidolon* (image-at-large, the *Bild*-at-large of the *Einbildungskraft*, the Imagination). However, the *specific* nature of this kind of image is to be located in the context of Kant's distinction between productive and reproductive Imagination (since the figurative synthesis is achieved by the productive Imagination), which parallels Plato's notorious distinction (e.g., in *Soph.* 236a–b) between *eikon* and *phantasma* and, of course, anticipates Coleridge's no less notorious distinction between "imagination" and "fancy," two terms "joined with accidents of translation from original works of different countries."[15] The former term qualifies the mimetic, sensible product of the *eide*, and so reproduction. The latter term, instead, is used in connection with an autonomous productive power proper, a product of the *phantasia*. As long as it is synthetically *produced* by the

Imagination, the inner sense, for Kant, as a necessary figure "of the diverse of sensible intuition," is therefore phantastically produced.

Analogously, the expression "synthesis of the productive Imagination" appears to figuratively unite two disparate families of implications: on one hand, the contingency as well as the relative indeterminacy of production; on the other, the "a priori possible and necessary" nature of production itself. If the latter implication points indeed to the necessary *Zusammenfließen* of concepts and objects, and so to the "synthetic influence of the Understanding on the inner sense [*synthetischer Einfluß des Verstandes auf den inneren Sinn*]," the former implication suggests that all synthesis of the productive Imagination is achieved in a contingent mode, so to speak, and can never be in fact more than a subdued synthesis, a hyposynthesis proper. Here again there seems to be a close relation between the *productive* Imagination and the Reason, as in both cases it is a question of "a faculty *through which* first begins the sensorial condition of an empirical series of effects [*ein Vermögen, durch welches die sinnliche Bedingung einer empirische Reihe von Wirkungen zuertst anfängt*]" (B580). Hypo-synthetical *Verstehen* (as the attribution of inner sense) is thus properly defined as the *cause* of its objects, or, rather, as the heuristic fiction of their very cause: the figure of otherwise unknowable objects, the fictional and necessary (i.e., the necessarily fictional) species of nonexistent genera.

The consideration of the inner sense as an effect of the Understanding (and ultimately as an effect of the Reason) is indeed the central consequence of the famed Kantian metaphor of the Copernican Revolution,[16] According to this metaphor, "we ourselves bring to phenomena the order and the regularity which we call nature" (A125); that is, "we can know a priori only about things what we ourselves have put there" (B, p. xviii). Hence the conclusion, at the end of the "Transcendental Analytic," that the Understanding's accomplishment (indeed, its only accomplishment) is "to anticipate [*zu antizipieren*] the form of a possible experience in general" (B303).

Concerning this problem, the crucial position of Kant's doctrine of the Imagination (specifically, of the productive Imagination, discussed above) is that the Imagination is conceived as the faculty that grounds the possibility of our "a priori prescribing laws to nature as the embodiment [*Inbegriffe*] of all phenomena" (B163). It is, as Kant calls it, "the connecting faculty [*das verknüpfende Vermögen*]" (B164). Thus the double subjection of the Imagination, both to the Understanding and to the Sensibility (ibid.), and the specific nature of its products. Indeed, nowhere does Kant suggest that either intuitions or concepts are produced by the Imagination. Kant's suggestion, as well as his theory on the productive Imagination, is rather that the Imagination produces a link between intuitions and concepts. This link is the figurative synthesis proper, figuration being here the power both to mediate and to inscribe the specific trace of all figuration *in* figuration (what I called above "hypo-synthesis"). Figuration is therefore a figment of the productive Imagination, as Kant's doctrine of the Reason—which is simultaneously a theory on the purely pragmatic role of Reason as well as a theory of fiction—in the "Transcendental Dialectic," continually asserts. According to such theories (Kant remarks apropos "the concept of a higher intelligence"), "a mere idea" is

> only [*nur*] the scheme of the concept of a thing in general, arranged after the conditions of the highest unity of Reason [*der größten Vernunfteinheit*] and serving only [*nur*] for preserving [*um . . . zu erhalten*] the highest systematic unity in the empirical use of our reason, while it is as

if [*gleichsam*] one derives the object of experience from the imaginary object of that idea [*von dem eingebildeten Gegenstande dieser Idee*], as if it were its ground or cause. (B698)

I have my doubts as to the task of "preserving the highest systematic unity in the empirical use of our reason" (and so does Kant, at least judging from his use of *nur*), in the sense that, after Wittgenstein, I believe that language usually takes care of it in a satisfactory manner. Be that as it may, what is remarkable in Kant's remark is that such a preservation is *simultaneously* achieved "as if [*gleichsam*]" by the derivation of "the object of experience from the imaginary object of [an] idea [*von dem eingebildeten Gegenstande ‹einer› Idee*]": that is, by the purely *eingebildete* supposition of a ground.

The passage above, therefore, indicates a particular mode of interference of "die größte Vernunfteinheit" (the highest unity of Reason) and the Imagination—namely the power to produce *eingebildete* objects. This interference very much goes against the commonplaces of Kantian commentary which tend to insist on the extraterritoriality (both to praise it and to damn it) of the Imagination vis-à-vis the empirical and the theoretical.[17] Indeed, it suggests that the empirical use of Reason is made possible by the Imagination, just as it suggests that there is no place for the Imagination (let alone in an aesthetics) apart from both Reason and experience.

And then, of course, there is Kant's remark as a whole, and the problem of knowing what kind of remark that is. Kant's own answer would be that it is a *critical* remark. I take it to be, instead, an unintentional remark on the limits of criticism. In fact, critical philosophy seems to be forever bound to remain a subdued analysis of the fiction of interpretation (that is, a reiteration of the produced nature of all links), as opposed to either the dogmatic dream of a natural contiguity between faculties (which, ironically enough, gave us the dream of a meaningful culture and of a philosophy of history) or the skeptical hope of doing away with figuration altogether (and so restoring yet again a seamless solipsistic contiguity between faculties). That the overcoming of criticism can be achieved only dogmatically or skeptically shows both how powerful Kant's meta-description of philosophy is, and how much such a description necessarily is a description of the roots of invention.

Postscript: That Book

That book, the book you have just read, or the book you perhaps have not read at all, ends without a noticeable conclusion wherefrom readers could extract and summarize the results arrived at. In the Introduction, I indirectly suggested why such a conclusion would not belong in the structure of the argument. The book above, while by no means being a motley collection of pieces, consists mainly of three long essays whose resemblances and differences as discussed in the Introduction are summarized in the title. In the process of writing it, I had to reread it many times, to a point where all general ideas vanished from my mind. Not without some measure of relief, I put the manuscript aside. While preparing it for publication, I had, alas, to read it once more (and perhaps for the last time). I then noticed a curious feature of the three main chapters that I thought could attenuate some of the predictable difficulties for its readership.

I believe a likely cause for such difficulties has to do with the obvious differences between the three texts discussed. The first text, Wilde's *De Profundis*, probably will be more familiar to persons who have studied literature. Some of these, nevertheless, will resent a few philosophical niceties in the analysis. Others will deplore the obvious lack of expressions of affection for the text or for its author, expressions with which literary types usually cannot dispense. The third text, Kant's *Critique of Pure Reason*, mostly will be familiar to persons with a philosophical education, who might, however, not recognize the text they once read in my discussion of it. I am not, of course, implying that my discussion is sublimely incommensurable with what usually is said about that text, only suggesting that my commentary throws in terms and tricks that readers who have studied literature, rather than philosophy, are more likely to recognize. Because, unfortunately, people tend not to take in an equally serious way the *B*'s and the *P*'s in their libraries (*grosso modo* philosophy and literature), some discomfort could be expected. The second text, Nietzsche's *The Birth of Tragedy*, is one of the very few texts that usually are part of the curriculum of both *B* people and *P* people. The former will miss references to the context of the history of Western metaphysics and perspectivism. The latter will regret the lack of references to Euripides and German late Romanticism. Most, perhaps, will deem my discussion otiose or plain wrong.

All appearances notwithstanding, the prospect of a hermeneutic comedy of errors whereby, for each text, those who might have read the book would be those who might not understand its discussion, and vice versa, is not a pleasant one to me. Nothing, of course, can replace knowledge of the texts. Should this book lead someone into reading at least one of the three main texts for the first time, I would find it to be amply justified. Indeed, I never was able to write more than an occasional short article about texts I despise.

The feature that I now retrospectively realize the three main chapters have in common is simple enough: they all discuss texts in an upside-down sort of way. The case of Kant, in Chapter 4, is perhaps the easiest to understand, as well as the least momentous.

In my discussion of the *Critique of Pure Reason*, I claim that, in the "Transcendental Logic" (which comprises some 90 percent of the work), its second part (or "Transcendental Dialectic") contains a powerful redescription of its first part, the so-called Transcendental Analytic. This would not be a particularly exciting fact if it weren't for two additional circumstances. The first is that such redescription is at odds with some important points in the Analytic. The second is that the Analytic is usually taken to contain all there is to know in the first *Critique*. This feature is not due to a crucial mistake by Kant that many generations of commentators blindly have disregarded and that I finally have exposed. It is, I believe, rather due to Kant's uneasiness about his own explanation in the Analytic of how we produce knowledge. Reading the text backward appeared therefore to be in order, even at the price of losing the sense of the text's structure that has earned the praise of many readers. If one adds to this fact the notion, intermittently developed by Kant himself in the Dialectic, that the best way to describe knowledge is by starting at its very end, the fact that its objects are produced, one perhaps will realize how the chosen form of reading is related to Kant's description of human knowledge, at least in the latter part of the first *Critique*.

In Chapter 2, I insist that the text must be read against the explicit advice of its author. Wilde presents his own letter as a classic case of spontaneous overflow of powerful feelings, "blotted in many places with tears, in some with the signs of passion or pain," and urges us to "take it as it stands . . . blots, corrections, and all." The state of the manuscript, however, testifies rather to a classic case of emotion recollected in tranquillity, albeit in the dubious tranquillity of Reading Gaol. Part of it, at least, appears to be a fair copy of a lost previous version, and the whole of the manuscript suggests that, contrary to what Wilde says, he had at all times considerable amounts of paper at his disposal. I recall these well-known facts not in order to add insult to injury and detract from the quality of the letter. Rather, I think they corroborate, against Wilde's intention, a theory that Wilde expressed in the same letter, according to which "whatever is first in feeling comes away last in form." Instead of doing what is usually done with the letter, then, and granting at the outset that it is an expression of the feelings, emotions, and experiences of a person under difficult circumstances for whom the only literary problem was that of adjusting his command of the language to the magnitude of his misfortunes, I take the latter formula (and Wilde as a critic) seriously. I thus follow the doctrine according to which these circumstances have been produced by literature, have come away as form, if only to suggest that no one, not even Wilde, ultimately can make that hysteron proteron work. Producing the facts of the matter is the sort of thing writers dream about, not the sort of thing writers can do.

These last words also apply to Nietzsche's *The Birth of Tragedy*, or, to be precise, to the series of texts that are now published under that title. Since its third edition, the work has been reprinted with an "Attempt at Self-Criticism" as a preface in which Nietzsche says in so many words that this is a failed book, and a bad book at that. There are, of course, more such cases. (Wittgenstein's preface to the *Investigations* comes to mind.) Unlike those, however, Nietzsche's "Attempt," while presenting itself as a critical supplement to the original work, tries to redescribe that work in terms that amount to a full-fledged correction of the work as a whole. Curiously enough, this sort of tension already is prefigured in the first edition of the text, where the latter part of the book (roughly the last ten sections) attempts to correct an explanation offered in the earlier part of the

book. This earlier narrative suggests that Greek tragedy is irretriev-
ably dead and gone. Without any special notice, it is followed by a
triumphant resurrection of Greek tragedy in the form of Wagnerian
opera. The narrative about the emergence of Wagnerian opera,
therefore, is another critical supplement to a previous narrative. It
would seem that the history of Nietzsche's book merely shows the
possibility of correction and rewriting at work. As with Wilde,
however, this description is not quite accurate. Indeed, each
successive correction awkwardly tends to refer back to previous
corrections, because it can acquire its intelligibility only from the
text it purports to supersede. This infinite regression, I think, easily
could be extended to the preliminary drafts of the book, and
perhaps to a point in time at which there was no intention of writing
such a book.

Whereas in the case of Wilde I suggest we examine claims of
pristine sincerity, in the case of Nietzsche I suggest we examine
claims of infinite correctability. Only apparently are these opposed.
In fact, both claims typify the belief in the possibility of absolute
beginnings, beginnings intentionally produced by a special class of
persons (e.g., poets or philosophers)—in short, the possibility of
invention of (what I call) the matter of the facts. However, such a
possibility, or so I argue, never quite materializes.

That book, finally, the book you have just read, will read, or have
just given up reading, has been a long time in the making. It was first
developed in a series of seminars at the Program in Literary Theory
and the Romance Literatures Department of the University of
Lisbon between 1990 and 1992. The discussions in these seminars
have proven to be crucial to its development, and I am naturally very
grateful to all participants. Sections of it were presented occasional-

ly as lectures since 1994, both in Europe and in the United States. For reasons of brevity, and not without regret, a few texts were dropped from the original project, namely Poe's "The Imp of the Perverse" and Italo Svevo's *La Coscienza di Zeno*.

Several people have been patient enough to offer their opinion and advice or. parts and on the whole of the manuscript throughout the several stages of its composition, and in its ever decreasing dimensions: Brett Bourbon, Claus Clüver, António Feijó, Maria de Lourdes Ferraz, Hans Ulrich Gumbrecht, and the readers for Stanford University Press. The text has much benefited also from the suggestions and emendations of Bud Bynack, Paul Psoinos, and Helen Tartar.

Ana and, after 1995, Madalena, have been behind it all.

Notes

Notes

Introduction

1. Jürgen Habermas, "Der Universalitätsanspruch der Hermeneutik" (1970), Engl. transl. J. Bleicher, in idem, *Contemporary Hermeneutics: Hermeneutics as Method, Philosophy and Critique* (London: Routledge, 1980), pp. 181–211.

2. Georges Gusdorf, *Les Origines de l'herméneutique* (Paris: Payot, 1988), pp. 19–39.

3. Manfred Frank, "Die Grenzen der Beherrschbarkeit der Sprache: Das Gespräch als Ort der Differenz zwischen Neostrukturalismus und Hermeneutik," partial English transl. Richard Palmer, in Diane P. Michelfelder and Richard E. Palmer, eds., *Dialogue & Deconstruction: The Gadamer-Derrida Encounter* (Albany: SUNY Press, 1984), p. 152.

4. Ibid., p. 153.

5. Ibid.

6. This topic deserves some attention in *Friends of Interpretable Objects* (Cambridge, Mass.: Harvard University Press, forthcoming).

Chapter 1

1. Leo Spitzer, "Das Eigene und das Fremde: Über Philologie und Nationalismus," *Die Wandlung*, 1:7 (1946), 576–94, 593.

2. Stanley Fish, *Doing What Comes Naturally: Change, Rhetoric, and the Practice of Theory in Literary and Legal Studies* (Oxford: Clarendon Press, 1989), p. 411.

3. Lewis Carroll, *Through the Looking-Glass and What Alice Found*

There, in *The Complete Works of Lewis Carroll* (New York: Modern Library, 1936), chap. 6, p. 214.

4. Hilary Putnam, "A Comparison of Something with Something Else," *New Literary History*, 17:1 (1985), 61–79, esp. 76.

5. The locus classicus is in David Hume's *A Treatise of Human Nature*, bk. 3, pt. 1, chap. 1 ("Moral Distinctions Not Deriv'd from Reason"): "In every system of morality, which I have hitherto met with, I have always remark'd, that the author proceeds for some time in the ordinary way of reasoning, and establishes the being of a God, or makes observations concerning human affairs; when of a sudden I am surpriz'd to find, that instead of the usual copulations of propositions, *is*, and *is not*, I meet with no proposition that is not connected with an *ought*, or an *ought not*. This change is imperceptible; but is, however, of the last consequence. For as this *ought*, or *ought not*, expresses some new relation or affirmation, 'tis necessary that it shou'd be observ'd and explain'd; and at the same time that a reason should be given, for what seems altogether inconceivable, how this new relation can be a deduction from others, which are entirely different from it. But as authors do not commonly use this precaution, I shall presume to recommend it to the readers; and am persuaded, that this small attention wou'd subvert all the vulgar systems of morality."

6. Martin Heidegger, *Sein und Zeit* (1927; reprint, Tübingen: Niemeyer, 1986), sect. 32, p. 148.

Chapter 2

1. Ralph Waldo Emerson, "The American Scholar: An Oration Delivered Before the Phi Beta Kappa Society, at Cambridge, August 31, 1837," in *The Complete Prose Works of Ralph Waldo Emerson* (London: Ward, Lock and Co., n.d.), p. 333.

2. This is perhaps why so-called realist writing depends so much on the idea of a thematics—that is, on a previously available collection of putative subjects allegedly independent from and previous to language.

3. A full description of the manuscript can be found, for instance, in Paul Zumthor's preface to his translation of *Abélard et Héloïse: Correspondance* (Paris: UGE, 1979), pp. 7–40, esp. pp. 7–12.

4. The letter, written in the Reading Gaol between January and March

1897, was published first in 1905 by Robert Ross in a very reduced version as *De Profundis* and then, in a slightly longer version, in 1908, in *The Collected Edition of the Works of Oscar Wilde*, ed. R. Ross (London: Methuen). The manuscript was presented by Ross to the British Museum in 1909 and put on hold for fifty years. In 1949 Vyvyan Holland (Wilde's youngest son) published the first "complete edition" (always as *De Profundis*), based on one of the two typed copies that Ross had had made, at Wilde's request, in 1897. (The *second* copy, incidentally, was apparently sent to Douglas, who has always claimed that he never received it.) After its release, the manuscript was published in full (as "To Lord Alfred Douglas") by Sir Rupert Hart-Davis in his *The Letters of Oscar Wilde* (London: Hart-Davis, 1962). Sir Rupert restored over a thousand words omitted by Ross from the typescript ("almost all of them fiercely critical of Douglas and his father") and corrected several hundred errors: "misreadings of Wilde's hand . . . aural misprints . . . Ross's 'improvement' of Wilde's grammar and syntax . . . the inexplicable shifting of passages and whole paragraphs from one part of the letter to another." See Rupert Hart-Davis, ed., *Selected Letters of Oscar Wilde* (Oxford: Oxford University Press, 1989), pp. 152–53 note. (In this chapter I use the text as reprinted there, pp. 152–240. All further page references to this edition are included in the text.)

Sir Rupert's analysis of the manuscript shows, moreover, that, contrary to what Wilde declares in the letter, the text was considerably reworked and rewritten: for example, of the twenty four-page folio sheets which contain the text, three "have every appearance of being fair copies" (p. 153 n.), and eighteen of the twenty folios do not finish at the end of a sentence.

As for the alternative title, *Epistola: In carcere et vinculis*, it was suggested ("it may be spoken of as . . .") by Wilde to Ross in a letter of April 1, 1897 (cf. Hart-Davis 1989, p. 242), but never adopted. (Ross preferred to follow the *De Profundis* suggestion, made by E. V. Lucas.) According to Richard Ellmann, Wilde's suggestion probably alludes to W. S. Blunt's prison poems ("prison has had an admirable effect on Mr. Wilfrid Blunt as a poet," Wilde wrote while reviewing them, in 1889), entitled *In Vinculis*: cf. Ellmann, *Oscar Wilde* (Harmondsworth: Penguin, 1988), pp. 479–85, esp. p. 479; and "The Critic as Artist as Wilde," in idem, ed., *The Artist as Critic: The Critical*

Writings of Oscar Wilde (Chicago: University of Chicago Press, 1969), pp. xxiii–xxiv.

5. A. Ernout and A. Meillet, *Dictionnaire étymologique de la langue latine: Histoire des mots*, 3d ed. (Paris: Klincksieck, 1951).

6. Ibid., vol. 1, pp. 153–54, s.v. "calamitas," "calamus."

7. Cf. Walt Whitman's (equally calamitous) definition of *calamus* (the famous title of one of the sections of *Leaves of Grass*) in a November 1867 letter to M. D. Conway: "'Calamus' is a common word here. It is the very large aromatic grass, or rush, growing about water-ponds in the valleys . . . grows all over the Northern and Middle States—see Webster's Large Dictionary—Calamus—definition 2." Definition 2, however, as Francis Murphy remarks, reads "in antiquity, a pipe or fistula, a wind instrument, made of a reed or oaten stalk" (Murphy, ed., *The Complete Poems of Walt Whitman* [Harmondsworth: Penguin, 1986], p. 799 n.). The seemingly irrelevant and easily correctable *lapsus calami* ("Whitman may have had in mind Webster's *fourth* definition of the word," writes Murphy), however, produces a perfect allegorical calamity: "antiquity" "all over the Northern and Middle States" or a "wind instrument" "growing about water-ponds."

8. Mark C. Taylor, *Tears* (Albany: SUNY Press, 1990), p. 228.

9. A lapidary instance of this use can be found in Martin Heidegger, *Der Ursprung des Kunstwerkes* (1950; reprint, Stuttgart: Reclam, 1982), p. 10: "Mit dem angefertigen Ding wird im Kunstwerk noch etwas Anderes zusammengebracht. Zusammenbringen heißt griechisch *sumballein*. Das Werk ist Symbol." (Published in English as *Poetry, Language, Thought*, transl. A. Hofstadter [New York: Harper, 1975], p. 20: "In the work of art something other is brought together with the thing that is made. To bring together is, in Greek, *sumballein*. The work is a symbol.")

10. Ibid.: Ger. p. 63; Engl. p. 63.

11. Stretching our paragrammatic talents a bit, we can see with relatively little effort the *kalamos* lurking in the instinct. So the unattested verb *instingo* (whence the past participle *instinctus*), meaning "prick with a small stick," i.e., prick with a *calamus* or in-calamitize. Cf. *Oxford English Dictionary* s.v. "instinct"; Ernout and Meillet (above, n. 5) s.v. "stingo."

12. Just as Whitman's taking of the *calamus* in "What Think You I Take My Pen in Hand?" (the calamitous poem of *calamus*, if ever there was one),

designed "to record" a previous "record" ("two simple men I saw to-day on the pier . . . parting the parting of dear friends"), depends on a previous event. In this seemingly simple structure, however, the past tableau (*I* seeing two men on the pier) is always a double one (*I* taking my pen in hand to record *I* seeing two men on the pier): as soon as, to use Wilde's terms, the *I* becomes "dominated by you," it produces a past event, and thus a relation between writer and vision. Such is the calamity, whose structure of duplication and correspondence one should be careful to balance against Whitman's (as well as Wilde's) general insistence on all sorts of paths untrodden. Cf., e.g., Whitman's remark to Wilde (quoted in Ellmann, *Oscar Wilde* [above, n. 4], p. 161) in the first of their two meetings: "I aim at making my verse look all neat and pretty on the page, like the epitaph on a square tombstone."

13. Some pages earlier (p. 170), one finds a very literal illustration of how perversity follows from paradox and not the other way around:

> One day you come to me and ask me, as a personal favour to you, to write something for an Oxford undergraduate magazine, about to be started by some friend of yours, whom I have never heard of in all my life, and knew nothing at all about. To please you—what did I not do always to please you?—I sent him a page of paradoxes destined originally for the *Saturday Review*. A few months later I find myself standing in the dock of the Old Bailey on account of the character of the magazine.

Not only does "a page of paradoxes" lead (through a somewhat perverse metonymical chain) to the Old Bailey, but also the active construction ("I sent him") associated with a control over paradox production is replaced, as soon as the former "lord of language" (p. 186) gets to the Old Bailey, by a construction in which the agent becomes the object ("I find myself") whereby the consequences of a linguistic product are described as unintended. The same structure is reiterated in one of the most recurrent accusations to Lord Douglas—e.g., "That you were the true author of the hideous tragedy did not occur to you" (p. 177)—as well as in the metaphysical hypothesis concerning the motivation of Douglas's own actions: "It makes me feel sometimes as if you yourself had been merely a puppet worked by some secret and unseen hand to bring terrible events to a terrible issue" (p. 172).

14. Synchronicity is, of course, asserted in many different ways and vocabularies—e.g., the series of musical metaphors that invariably assert the superposition of past and present, just as they assert the coincidence of life and art, and memory and event, in the mode of symbolic (and symphonic) necessity:

> My friendship with you, in the way through which I am forced to remember it, appears to me always as a prelude consonant with those varying modes of anguish which each day I have to realise; nay more, to necessitate them even; as though my life . . . had all the while been a real Symphony of Sorrow, passing through its rhythmically-linked movements to its certain resolution, with that inevitableness that in Art characterises the treatment of every great theme. (p. 165)

The control of the suffering subject over the past is what is precisely assured by a principle of availability of the past to memory through the coincidence between past and present. Memory is what is capable of *causing* past (in the special sense cf being capable to put past to a use) by constructing "consonances" and coming "to necessitate them even." The temporality of the symbol corresponds thus to the "symphony of sorrow" (more about sorrow in the next section), which cannot help but configure the present as a necessary repetition in which it is a priori guaranteed the "consonance" between "prelude" and "resolution." This is, indeed, the kind of past in which, as Nietzsche put it, "one would like to originate," as the present in question is the kind of present which is produced as a "certain resolution" of a "great theme."

15. The examples in the passage, from which the expressions that follow in the text are taken, are *The Happy Prince, The Young King, The Picture of Dorian Gray, The Critic as Artist, The Soul of Man Under Socialism, Salomé*, and the prose poem "The Artist."

16. Interestingly enough, one of the Latin designations for anastrophe is precisely *perversio* (cf. H. Lausberg, *Elemente der literarischen Rhetorik* [Munich: Max Hüber, 1963], §330), which would perhaps reinforce the relationship between "paradox" and "perversion" in the preceding section as a relation between semantic and syntactic figures of reversal. "Life," in this sense, would have no meaning, only a syntax—no catastrophes, only anas-

trophes. The literary metaphors of irreversibility (e.g., "life as tragedy"), then, could perhaps be replaced here by literary metaphors of reversibility (e.g., "life as a farce").

17. There is a not immediately obvious sense in which the following remark by Emerson (*pace* both Emerson and Wilde) anticipates, derides, and eventually *confirms* Wilde's remark: "There are moods in which we court suffering, in the hope that here, at least we shall find reality, sharp peaks and edges of truth. But it turns out to be scene-painting and counterfeit. The only thing grief has taught me, is to know how shallow it is. That, like all the rest, plays about the surface, and never introduces me into the reality, for contact with which, we would even pay the costly price of sons and lovers" ("Experience," *Complete Prose Works* [above, n. 1], p. 103). In fact, for Emerson, just as for Wilde, the only thing that can be taught about grief is that it is "scene-painting." "The surface," in strict Wildean orthodoxy, is there the only beauty of sorrow, what comes down last of it.

18. So, on the next page, Wilde writes: "Do not be afraid of the past. If people tell you that is irrevocable, do not believe them. The past, the present and the future are but one moment in the sight of God, in whose sight we should try to live. Time and space, succession and extension, are merely accidental conditions of Thought. The Imagination can transcend them, and more in a free sphere of ideal existences" (p. 239). The "Imagination" is here the symbolic (and syncretic) faculty par excellence, as the transcendence of time and space identifies with "the sight of God" as well as with the "free sphere of ideal existences." To "try to live" in the "sight of God," then, can mean only *reproducing* the sight of God and representing as "one moment" past, present, and future. The fear of the past as well as of any sense of irrevocability is thus literally overcome through a process of idealization where the specific trace of events is purportedly neutralized in a transtemporal colloquium.

19. Cf. previous note. However, ironically enough, the repeated failure of imagination is the closest analogue to what imagination could not obtain—namely a coincidence between past, present, and future—since it determines a priori, and automatically, that the future will take place as a sorrowful reenactment of a past. The adequate figure of the "sight of God," then, is the figure of the impossibility of bridging the "chasm"—i.e., of rep-

resenting the sight of God. In both cases (cf. previous note again) fear as an event is neutralized, either through idealization (the description of a state of things where fear has no place) or through trivialization (the description of a state of things where fear has the only place). In any case, there is no place for salvational history as a dialectics of an overcoming of fear (in a therapeutical version) or as a series of preemptive strikes against ever possible terrible events (in a prophylactic version).

20. E.g., "When I tell you that between the autumn of 1892 and the date of my imprisonment I spent with you and on you more than £5000 in actual money, irrespective of the bills I incurred, you will have some idea of the sort of life on which you insisted. Do you think I exaggerate? My ordinary expenses with you for any ordinary day in London—for luncheon, dinner, supper, amusements, hansoms and the rest of it—ranged from £12 to £20, and the week's expenses were naturally in proportion and ranged from £80 to £130. For our three months at Goring my expenses (rent of course included) were £1340. Step by step with the Bankruptcy Receiver I had to go over every item of my life. It was horrible. *'Plain living and high thinking'* was, of course, an ideal you could not at that time have appreciated, but such an extravagance was a disgrace to both of us. One of the most delightful dinners I remember ever having had is one Robbie and I had together in a little Soho café, which cost about as many shillings as my dinners to you used to cost pounds. Out of my dinner with Robbie came the first and best of all my dialogues. Idea, title, treatment, mode, everything was struck out at a 3 franc 50 c. *table-d'hôte*. Out of the reckless dinners with you nothing remains but the memory that too much was eaten and too much was drunk" (p. 157). Also, e.g., much later in the text: "When I used to suggest that your mother should supply you with the money you wanted, you always had a very pretty and graceful answer. You said that the income allowed her by your father—some £1500 a year I believe—was quite inadequate to the wants of a lady of her position, and that you could not go to her for more money than you were getting already" (p. 229).

21. Cf. later in the same paragraph: "Of seed-time or harvest, of the reapers bending over the corn, or the grape-gatherers threading through the vines, of the grass in the orchard made white with broken blossoms or strewn with fallen fruit, we know nothing, and can know nothing" (ibid.).

22. An important ingredient in the whole process is the not so veiled allusion to *Hamlet*, I, v, where, of course, the Ghost, "forbid / To tell the secrets of my prison-house," precedes the tale of his own death by a reference to his manner of writing ("I could a tale unfold whose lightest word / Would harrow up thy soul"). Stretching it a bit, one could even say that among the intended effects of storytelling, described at some length by the Ghost in relation to Hamlet, is even a very literal confusion of spheres ("Make thy two eyes, like stars, start from their spheres").

23. And yet the notion that "where there is Sorrow there is holy ground" (p. 188) is the motto for the narration of a small incident protagonized by a character who can "realise it." Such a character, Robbie, "when I was brought down from my prison to the Court of Bankruptcy . . . waited in the long dreary corridor, that before the whole crowd, whom an action so sweet and simple hushed into silence, he might gravely raise his hat to me, as handcuffed and with bowed head I passed him by" (ibid.). And the narrator adds: "I have never said one single word to him about what he did. . . . It is not a thing for which one can render formal thanks in formal words. I store it in the treasury-house of my heart. I keep it there as a secret debt that I am glad to think I can never possibly repay" (ibid.). This narrated incident contains the double and contradictory destiny of sorrow. On the one hand it is an incident that, as told, portrays its adequate symbolic correlate as both a silent action and a silent debt, a "holy ground." On the other hand, by being told, it becomes the emblem of a discourse on the narrative posterity of sorrow, and necessarily desacralizes the ground of sorrow. The "debt" is thus paid as an annihilation of the meaning imputed to it, in a different currency, at it were.

Chapter 3

1. Friedrich Nietzsche (1872), *Die Geburt der Tragödie aus dem Geiste der Musik*, reprinted (1886) as *Die Geburt der Tragödie, oder: Griechentum und Pessimismus* and including the preface mentioned below in the text. Page numbers in this chapter refer, in this order, to the German text (including original spelling) in G. Colli and M. Montinari's critical edition of Nietzsche's collected works, *Sämtliche Werke: Kritische Studienausgabe* (Berlin and New York: De Gruyter, 1980), 1: 9–156; and to Walter Kauf-

mann's English translation in *The Birth of Tragedy and the Case of Wagner* (New York: Vintage, 1967), pp. 15–144. Changes (sometimes substantial) have been made in the translation.

2. Both when it is said that the book "seems to defend a well-rounded thesis, supported by relevant argument and illustration" and when it is said that "the text is held together by the pseudo-polarity of the Apollo/Dionysos dialectic that allows for a well-ordered teleology, because the ontological cards have been stacked from the beginning." Cf. Paul de Man, *Allegories of Reading* (New Haven: Yale University Press, 1979), p. 83. Even when there are substantial disagreements (and especially when such is the case), all that is written in this chapter is deeply indebted to Paul de Man's masterly study on *The Birth of Tragedy*, now chapter 4 in *Allegories of Reading*.

3. So Richard Wagner is referred to in the preface as "my sublime predecessor [*Vorkämpfer*, "pioneer"] on this path." Of course, in the terms of this preface there cannot be any "sublime" predecessors, in that the preface has to measure their achievements by its own standards. Thus, to use Kant's convenient distinction, predecessors can be only beautiful.

4. Alexander Nehamas, "Friedrich Nietzsche," in M. Groden and M. Kreiswirth, eds., *The Johns Hopkins Guide to Literary Theory and Criticism* (Baltimore: Johns Hopkins University Press, 1993), p. 546. In his *Nietzsche: Life as Literature* (Cambridge: Harvard University Press, 1985), Nehamas relates the function of the tragic chorus to a "most powerful representation of the vanity of all effort . . . assuring its spectators that even in their efforts to change nature, the tragic heroes, like those spectators themselves, are its products and elements" (p. 119).

5. E.g., *Ursprung und Ziel der Tragödie: Eine ästhetische Abhandlung, mit einem Vorwort an Richard Wagner* ("Origin and Aim of Tragedy: An Aesthetical Essay, with Preface Dedicated to Richard Wagner"), ed. Colli and Montinari (above, n. 1), vol. 7 (in the *Nachgelassene Fragmente* [1870–71]). Quotation from p. 7.

6. Hence the incomprehension of some Greek scholars such as Ulrich von Wilamowitz-Moellendorff, who complained right after the publication of the book about Nietzsche's scholarly "ignorance." Indeed, if *The Birth of Tragedy* is understood as a historical description followed by a somewhat eccentric (and irrelevant) appendix, the verdict cannot help being rather

negative. The ironic title of Wilamowitz's *Streitschrift*, however, "Zukunfts-philologie!" ("Philology of the Future!"), unwittingly translates something deeply at stake in Nietzsche's book—namely a reading (i.e., the production) of the future (rather than the description of a safe past).

7. The two major signs, of course, are what Nietzsche calls "German music" ("the vast solar orbit from Bach to Beethoven, from Beethoven to Wagner," 127, 119) and "German philosophy" (i.e., the project of transcendental philosophy—"the determination of limits" [128, 120]—undertaken by Kant and Schopenhauer). Both German music and German philosophy are said to arise "out of the Dionysian ground of the German spirit" (127, 119) as a power (*Macht*) which has "nothing in common with the originary conditions of Socratic culture" (ibid.).

8. So the metaphor of the future as an escape from captivity by the past translates not so much a metaphysical faith in liberation as the temporal discontinuity between past and future: what is hoped for is, so to speak, a discontinuity. Referring to the inevitability of a rebirth, Nietzsche produces the following (classical, alas!) analogy: "It is impossible that the divine strength of Herakles should languish forever in sumptuous bondage [*im üppigen Frohndienste*] to Omphale" (127, 119). Whereas the past attracts necessarily the "ample bondage" of accurate explanation (literally, here, it is the past of navel-inspecting, *omphaloskopia*, not very far away from the past of the second *Unzeitgemäße Betrachtung*), the future has to be made up by "divine strength." Such a discontinuity, I suspect, is what separates the first from the second part of the book, as the latter tells the story of the destruction of history through the force of an invented (and wholly fictional) future: specifically, a Dionysian one. The production of such an invention, however, is bound to vindicate the nature of the 1886 "self-criticism," in that it has to remain tentative, since, as Nietzsche does not fail to remark, the narrative of the "gradual awakening of the Dionysian spirit" depends wholly on the "classically instructive form" (128, 121) of "Hellenic analogies" (ibid.: this latter—crucial—passage will be discussed in detail further on in this section).

9. My allusion to Hegel's *Phenomenology* is to the very first chapter, "Certainty at the Level of Sense-Experience," which, as is well known, turns upon the possibility of a "mere apprehension [*Auffassen*] free from concep-

tual comprehension [*Begreiffen*]," even if "*certainty* . . . is really and admittedly the abstractest and the poorest kind of *truth*" (*The Phenomenology of Mind*, transl. J. B. Baillie [New York: Harper, 1967], pp. 149–60, esp. p. 149). Nietzsche's remark is from "The Birth of Tragedy" in *Ecce Homo* (*On the Genealogy of Morals* [and] *Ecce Homo*, transl. W. Kaufmann [New York: Vintage, 1969], p. 270).

10. Incidentally, the form of the problem seems to derive here from the form of a typical Darwinian metaphysical problem, namely that of reconciling the postulate concerning the evolution of the species with the agonistic postulate concerning the struggle for survival. Only apparently is the standard synthesis ("natural selection," an "unerring power . . . which selects exclusively for the good of each organic being") a solution. In fact, either (1) its conditions are to be known in advance, no indetermination exists in the struggle for survival, and we can speak of general a priori principles concerning the evolution of the species but cannot speak of any "struggle" except in an empirical way; or (2) its conditions are not known in advance, there is a factor of indetermination in the struggle for survival, and so "the evolution of species" is an empirical, a posteriori, description of a collection of phylogenetic victors. According to (1) and (2), respectively, "struggle for survival" and "the evolution of species" resemble nostalgic metaphors for biological impossibilia. (The quotation above is from "Abstract of a Letter from C. Darwin, Esq., to Prof. Asa Gray, Boston, U.S., dated Down, September 5th, 1857," in *The Collected Papers of Charles Darwin*, ed. P. H. Barrett (Chicago: University of Chicago Press, 1977), 2: 8.)

11. A "miracle" is here an aesthetic event proper, or, rather, this is why the *form* of this miracle is merely temporal and spatial (a "'now' in Greece") and is apprehended through intuitions. In fact, if there were (e.g.) a causal nexus to the appearance of Greek tragedy, such an appearance would be subsumable in concepts. By remaining confined to the sphere of the aesthetic, this miracle is literally unexplainable. The sense of Nietzsche's use of "aesthetic," however, even if it follows the post-Kantian (or, rather, the Baumgartner-Schillerian) definition of the aesthetic as the domain of art, is here, and primarily, Kantian: the aesthetic is the domain of sensibility, and so of intuition.

12. To the point that "metaphysischer Wunderakt" can be said to con-

tain both a "physisches Wunder" (a "physical wonder") and a "Meta-Akt."
Only a meta-act can effect a physical wonder.

13. Colli and Montinari, eds. (above, n. 1), 7: 179.

14. Vs., e.g., Freud's description of what he calls "compromise-forma-
tion [Kompromissbildung]" in chapter 23 of the Introductory Lectures to
Psycho-analysis (1916–17): "Die beiden Kräfte . . . treffen in Symptom
wieder zusammen, versöhnen sich gleichsam durch das Kompromiß der
Symptombildung" ("The two forces . . . meet again in the symptom and are
reconciled, as it were, by the compromise of symptom-construction)," in
Studienausgabe, ed. A. Mitscherlich, A. Richards, and J. Strachey (Frankfurt: Fischer, 1969), 1: 350.

15. For a general context of both episodes in Raphael's Transfiguration,
cf. Matthew 17:1–21 and Luke 9:28–50. For doctrinal symbolic implications see (e.g.) Aquinas's curious pleonasm in Summa Theologiae III.45.4.2:
transfiguration "est sacramentum secundae regenerationis [is the sacrament
of a second regeneration]" (my emphasis).

16. The problem is perhaps common to many (though by no means all)
contemporary rediscoverers of Kant's doctrine of the sublime, and indeed to
the very idea of a rediscovery of the sublime (or allegory, or otherness, or
difference). What in Kant's terms would be confusing the beautiful with the
sublime is paralleled there by the implication that such a rediscovery is
achieved through a particular (possibly new) more adequate intentional representation of an object. In short, the rehabilitated topics are construed as
the objects of a communicational act, and therefore transfigured. This is
why, in this sense, the sublime, allegory, otherness, and difference remain
thematic products of a specific (and recognizable) poetics, framed by universal principles of adequation. For the best recent sustained discussion—
known to me, at least—of a theoretical alternative (with intermittent references to Nietzsche on tragedy), see Wlad Godzich, The Culture of Literacy
(Cambridge, Mass.: Harvard University Press, 1994), pp. 25–33.

17. The reader will recognize here an allusion to Donald Davidson's famous 1978 essay "What Metaphors Mean" (reprinted in idem, Inquiries into
Truth and Interpretation [Oxford: Clarendon Press, 1984], pp. 245–64). Although I think that Davidson's account of metaphorical meaning is certainly
one of the most stimulating available ("metaphors mean what the words, in

their most literal interpretation, mean, and nothing more," p. 245)—even if I have some problems with phrases such as "most literal interpretation" (while endorsing Davidson's more general point that "the semantic features of words cannot be explained directly on the basis of non-linguistic phenomena" ("Radical Interpretation" [1973], *op. cit.*, p. 127)—my problem in this section *is not* Davidson's problem. Rather, I am interested in certain metaphors that do not have a meaning in a special sense: the special sense of not being *effective*, or, even better, the special case of metaphors built on tropes such as—to follow Lausberg's enumeration in his *Elemente der literarischen Rhetorik* (above, Chap. 2, n 16), §37.1—irony, emphasis, understatement, hyperbole, some cases of periphrasis, oxymoron, some cases of zeugma, or chiasmus. But then again, it might be the case that, *pace* myself, the discussion in the present section is still a discussion about what Davidson calls "the *effects* metaphors have on us" ("What Metaphors Mean," p. 261).

18. Even if Nietzsche's problem here does not appear to be Jacques Derrida's (viz. in the locus classicus of the latter's doctrine of the "supplément": *De la Grammatologie* [Paris: Minuit, 1967], p. 208), the term "nécessité" occurs in Derrida's discussion of the supplement and retrospectively allegorizes Nietzsche's problem: "Il y a une nécessité fatale, inscrite dans le fonctionnement même du signe, à ce que le substitut fasse oublier sa fonction de vicariance et se fasse passer pour la plénitude d'une parole dont il ne fait pourtant que *suppléer* la carence et l'infirmité. Car le concept de supplément—qui determine ici celui d'image représentative—abrite en lui deux significations dont la cohabitation est aussi étrange que nécessaire." ("A fateful necessity is inscribed within the very workings of the sign, in that the replacement causes its vicarious function to be forgotten and passes for the fullness of the word, whose shortcomings and impairment it was nevertheless supplementing. Indeed, the concept of 'supplement'—which determines that of the representational image here—conveys two meanings, whose coexistence is as strange as it is necessary.")

19. The whole passage rewrites a well-known antecedent in Plato's *Phaedo*, with interesting changes—for example, Nietzsche's "Sokrates, treibe musik!" ("Socrates, practice music!") corresponds to Plato's much more specific O *Sokrates, . . . mousiken poiei kai ergazou* ("Socrates, . . .

compose and practice music!"). Cf. *Phaedo*, transl. H. N. Fowler (Cambridge, Mass.: Harvard University Press, 1971), 60e.

20. Contrary to what happens in the *Phaedo*. In fact, Socrates is there far from being compelled by the vision (which, even if it is "the same dream," does present itself "sometimes in one form and sometimes in another," even if always "saying the same thing," 60e). Referring to his musical exercises, he casually remarks (in a "supplementary" tone): "I wished to test the meaning of certain dreams and to make sure I was neglecting no duty in case their repeated commands meant that I must cultivate the Muses in this way" (ibid.).

21. "But now, after the trial and while the festival of the god delayed my execution, I thought, in case the repeated dream really meant to tell me to make this which is ordinarily called music, I ought to do so and not to disobey. For I thought it was safer not to go hence before making sure that I had done what I ought, by obeying the dream and composing verses" (*Phaedo*, transl. Fowler, 61a–b).

Chapter 4

1. Any cursory search among titles of books in print (in English) will show that the expression *The Invention of* occurs many times, preceding such terms as (in alphabetical order) Africa, America, Ancient Israel, Appalachia, Argentina, Athens, Autonomy, Canada, Capitalism, Comfort, Communication, Culture, Dante's *Commedia*, Dionysus, Dolores del Rio, Ethiopia, Ethnicity, Fire, Free Labor, George Washington, Hebrew Prose, Heterosexuality, Ice Skating, Infinity, Journalism, Kindness, Liberty, Literary Subjectivity, Literature, Love, Memory, Nature, Politics in Colonial Malaya, Pornography, Primitive Society, Progress, Prophecy, Race, "Race," Scotland, Society, Sodomy, Solitude, Somalia, Spain, the Americas, the Renaissance Woman, the Self, the West, the White Race, and Tradition. *Inventions of*, furthermore, will be found to precede Difference, History, Monuments, and Reading, and *"Invention" of* occurs in *The "Invention" of the Queer*. To these I should add my personal favorite, the title of a book of poems which I unfortunately could not locate: *The Invention of the Afternoon Nap*.

2. The name that comes to mind is, of course, Hilary Putnam. See, e.g.,

his *Realism with a Human Face*, ed. J. Conant (Cambridge, Mass.: Harvard University Press, 1990), especially the chapter "A Defence of Internal Realism," pp. 30–42. By "realism," of course, I do not mean necessarily what Putnam calls *metaphysical* realism.

3. Nelson Goodman, "The Fabrication of Facts" in *Ways of Worldmaking* (Indianapolis: Hackett, 1978), pp. 91–107.

4. Ibid., p. 91.

5. Ludwig Wittgenstein, *Vermischte Bemerkungen*, ed. G. H. von Wright and H. Nyman (Frankfurt: Suhrkamp, 1977); transl. P. Winch, *Culture and Value* (Oxford: Blackwell, 1984), p. 39e.

6. Jacques Derrida, "Psyche: Inventions of the Other," transl. C. Porter, in L. Waters and W. Godzich, eds., *Reading de Man Reading* (Minneapolis: University of Minnesota Press, 1989), p. 25.

7. Immanuel Kant, *Kritik der reinen Vernunft*, ed. W. Weischedel, in *Werke in zwölf Bänden: Theorie-Werkausgabe* (Frankfurt: Suhrkamp, 1968), vols. 3 and 4, cited in the text of this chapter by the page number of the second edition (1787), preceded by the letter *B*. In some instances I comment on passages from the first edition (1781) which are absent from the second; the page numbers in those passages, according to common usage, I indicate with the letter *A*. All translations are my own.

8. Cf. Kant's famous remark (which has persisted as an anonymous dictum in the hermeneutic tradition down to Gadamer) in the beginning of the "Transcendental Dialectic" about Plato's use of the term "idea": "I will not involve myself here in a literary investigation to determine the meaning that the sublime philosopher attached to his expression. I remark only that it is not unusual, both in the current conversation and in the writings, and through the comparison of the thoughts expressed by an author on his object, to understand him better than himself, in that he did not sufficiently determine his concept and therefore has spoken or even thought against its own intention [*und dadurch bisweilen seiner eigenen Absicht entgegen redete, oder auch dachte*]" (B370).

9. The translation of "der Schein" in the "Transcendental Dialectic" as "the apparent" rather than as "the appearance" follows Kant's distinction between "die Erscheinung" and "der Schein" (B349–50). "Die Erscheinung" is there "what appears" (i.e., the phenomenon) as opposed to "der Schein,"

which, just like "truth" (*Wahrheit*) denotes a property of judgment, since "neither the understanding . . . nor the senses can by themselves err" (B350).

10. Such is one of the specific varieties of perverseness once described by Edgar Allan Poe: "Having thus fathomed, to his satisfaction, the intentions of Jehovah, out of these intentions . . . [the intellectual or logical man] built his innumerable systems of mind" ("The Imp of the Perverse," in *The Complete Tales and Poems of Edgar Allan Poe* [Harmondsworth: Penguin, 1989], p. 280).

11. Cf. Kant's remarks on "affinity" in the first version of the "Deduction of the Pure Concepts of the Understanding": "All phenomena are therefore continuously connected [*in einer durchgängigen Verknüpfung*], after necessary principles, in a *transcendental affinity* [*in einer* transzendentalen Affinität], of which the empirical [affinity] is mere consequence. It seems in fact very contradictory and surprising that nature is subject to our subjective principle of apperception and, moreover, that it should depend on it in its conformity to laws. However, if one thinks that this nature is nothing in itself but an embodiment of phenomena [*Inbegriff von Erscheinungen*], and so no thing-in-itself, but rather merely a multitude of representations of the mind [*eine Menge von Vorstellungen des Gemüts*], one should not wonder that we see in the radical faculty of all our knowledge [*in dem Radikalvermögen aller unser Erkenntnis*]—that is, in the transcendental apperception—that unity due to which alone it can be called the object of all possible experience: i.e., a nature" (A113–14). And, shortly afterwards: "This objective principle of all association of phenomena [*Assoziation der Erscheinungen*] I call *affinity*" (A122).

12. This point is well known in the post-Kantian literature and has inspired authors otherwise as different as Nietzsche, Simmel, and Vahinger to produce various theories of the *as-if*. In the discussion that follows, however, it is suggested that Kant's doctrines on hypothesis and synthesis cannot be assimilated easily to theories on necessary fictions.

13. The most famous postscript to the schematism of reason is to be found in Wittgenstein's preface to his *Philosophical Investigations*:

> After several unsuccessful attempts to weld my results together into such a whole, I realized that I should never succeed. The best that I

could write would never be more than philosophical remarks . . . and this was, of course, connected with the very nature of the investigation. For this compels us to travel over a wide field of thought crisscross in every direction.—The philosophical remarks in this book are, as it were, a number of sketches of landscapes. . . . The same or almost the same points were always being approached afresh from different directions, and new sketches made. Very many of these were badly drawn or uncharacteristic, marked by all the defects of a weak draughtsman. And when they were rejected a number of tolerable ones were left, which now had to be arranged and sometimes cut down, so that if you looked at them you could only get a picture of the landscape. Thus this book is really only an album.

Ludwig Wittgenstein, *Philosophische Untersuchungen*, ed. G. E. M. Anscome, R. Rhees, and G. H. von Wright (Oxford: Blackwell, 1953); transl. G. E. M. Anscombe, *Philosophical Investigations* (Oxford: Blackwell, 1981), p. vii.

14. Cf., e.g., "the synthesis is in general . . . the mere effect of the Imagination [*die bloße Wirkung der Einbildungskraft*]" (B103).

15. S. T. Coleridge, *Biographia Literaria or, Biographical Sketches of My Literary Life and Opinions* (1817), ed. G. Watson (London: Dent, 1956), 50.

16. The very first reference to Copernicus, in the preface to the second edition of the *Critique of Pure Reason* occurs precisely in the context of a hypothesis concerning the determining role of " 'our knowledge' vis-à-vis "the objects' ": "One should at least investigate once whether the tasks of metaphysics would not progress any better if we assume that objects should be ruled by our knowledge [*daß wir annhemen, die Gegenstände müssen sich nach unserem Erkenntnis richten*], which instead would be much more in accordance with the called-for possibility of an a priori knowledge, which would establish something concerning the objects prior to their being given to us. There is indeed here a similarity with the original thought of Copernicus, who, being unable to carry on the explanation of heavenly movement as long as he would admit that the whole host of stars was moving around the

observer, conjectured that it would yield a much better result if he were to make the observer move and leave the stars at rest" (B, p. xvi).

17. A good recent example of traditional commentary on what he calls "The Kantian Imaginary" is Terry Eagleton's eponymous chapter, in his otherwise merely uncomplicated *The Ideology of the Aesthetic* (Oxford: Blackwell, 1990), pp. 70–101. For Eagleton, drawing rather sparingly on Kantian texts (and a little too generously on commentators), "the imagination creates a purposive synthesis, but without feeling the need for a theoretical detour" (p. 85). Eagleton's imagination, after a crucial confusion—the kind of confusion that constitutes what Paul de Man, not Eagleton, called "the ideology of the aesthetic"—becomes, in his argument, synonymous with the aesthetic: "If the aesthetic yields us no knowledge, then, it proffers us something arguably deeper: the consciousness, beyond all theoretical demonstration, that we are at home in the world because the world is somehow mysteriously designed to suit our capacities. . . . [This] is the kind of heuristic fiction which permits us a sense of purposiveness, centredness and significance, and thus one which is of the very essence of the ideological" (ibid.). So his emphatic assertion according to which "the ideologico-aesthetic is that indeterminate region, stranded somewhere between the empirical and theoretical, in which abstractions seem flushed with irreducible specificity and accidental particulars raised to pseudo-cognitive status" (p. 95). Eagleton's description, however, applies remarkably well to what he takes his book to be, namely "a Marxist study" (p. 4).

Index

In this index an "f" after a number indicates a separate reference on the next page, and an "ff" indicates separate references on the next two pages. A continuous discussion over two or more pages is indicated by a span of page numbers, e.g., "57–59." *Passim* is used for a cluster of references in close but not consecutive sequence.